WALKS in the Cheviot Hills

A guide to fourteen walks of between
two-and-a-half and seven miles in length
in and around the Northumberland National Park

Produced and published by
Northumberland County Council
National Park and Countryside Department
Eastburn, South Park, Hexham, Northumberland.

Text by Joan Williams
Photographs by Karen Melvin
Designed and illustrated by Eric Dale

Old photographs of Wooler Bridge accident and
Wooler Fair loaned for reproduction by the
Cheviot Field Centre and Museum, Wooler.

ISBN 0 907632 00 9

Typesetting by Typeset (Newcastle) Limited, Killingworth, Newcastle upon Tyne.
Printed by John Thornton (Printers) Limited, Wallsend, Tyne and Wear.

Contents

WITH FOURTEEN 1:25000 (2½") MAPS

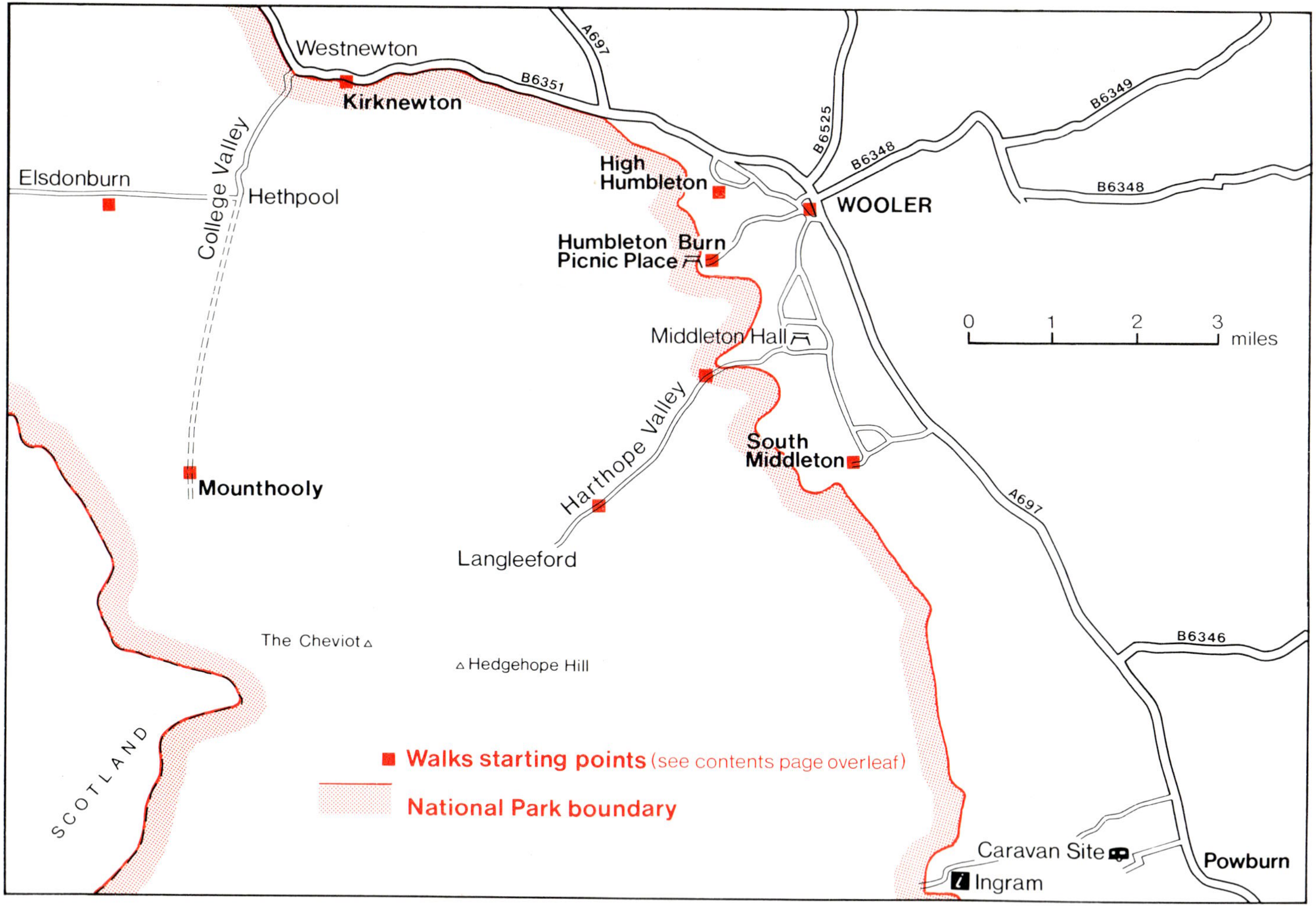

Westnewton
Kirknewton
B6351
A697
B6525
B6349
B6348
B6348
WOOLER
High Humbleton
Humbleton Burn Picnic Place
Elsdonburn
Hethpool
College Valley
Middleton Hall
South Middleton
Harthope Valley
Mounthooly
Langleeford
The Cheviot
Hedgehope Hill
0 1 2 3 miles
A697
B6346
Caravan Site
Ingram
Powburn
SCOTLAND
Walks starting points (see contents page overleaf)
National Park boundary

Introduction

THE NORTHUMBERLAND NATIONAL PARK is one of ten National Parks in England and Wales. It is not the largest, but within its elongated shape it contains as much, if not more variety of scenery as the larger National Parks.

It is the quality and variety of scenery within the Park that attracts so many walkers and enables visitors to feel a sense both of adventure and of solitude.

The Northumberland National Park Authority is unique in having countryside functions extending outside the Park boundaries. It can therefore help walkers to enjoy following paths outside as well as inside the Park. The combined work of the Authority's staff of National Park Wardens and Footpaths Officers has contributed largely to the walks described in this booklet being readily available.

The aim of this booklet is to provide both visitors and local people with walking routes that they can follow and with interesting information regarding things to see on the way. Whilst it is hoped that walkers will enjoy using the routes described it is also hoped that they will accept the responsibility that goes with using the countryside, and keep the Country Code. This means causing as little disturbance as possible to farm stock, keeping dogs under control, leaving gates as they find them and, of course, not leaving litter to mar the enjoyment of the next walker on the route.

Starting points and transport

There is adequate car parking space at the start of each walk in this booklet. Sometimes it will be a formal parking area with a hard surface whilst at others it will be a wide enough road verge to accommodate one or two cars at a time.

There are daily bus services between Newcastle and Wooler and between Alnwick and Wooler both of which pass or terminate within a reasonable walking distance of South Middleton or High Humbleton. There is a very limited 'Saturday only' service from Wooler via Kirknewton and Westnewton (for College Valley) and a school bus service which connects Wooler and Kirknewton on school days only.

National Parks in England and Wales

Some misconceptions surround the term 'National Park' because the Parks are not state owned and neither can they be compared with city parks; they also differ from the wild game National Parks of other countries. The nation may not own them, nor do we have unlimited rights of access over them, but they are certainly nationally recognised as areas of the highest quality scenery in England and Wales.

National Parks in this country came about as a result of Parliament passing the 'National Parks and Access to the Countryside Act' in 1949. The Act did not apply to Scotland which is why we talk only about the National Parks of England and Wales.

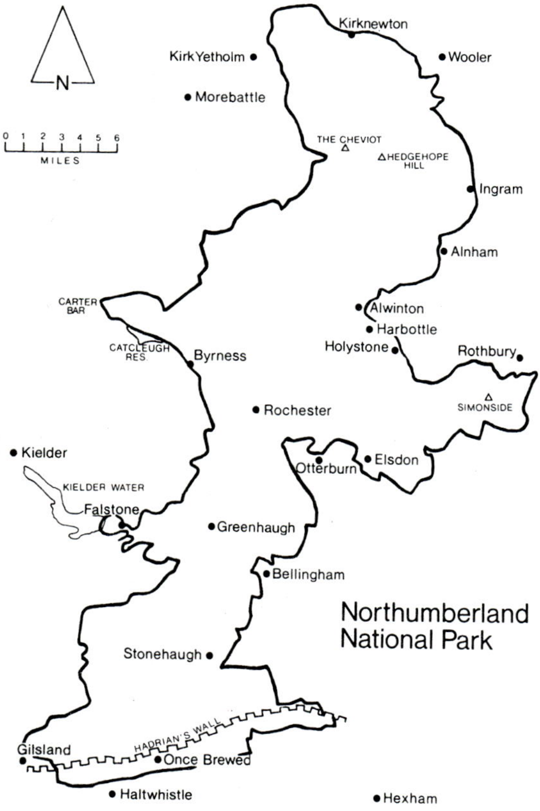

Selected as some of the finest remaining remote and open countryside – moor, mountain, valley and seashore – ten National Parks were designated between 1951 and 1957. They exist to safeguard particularly fine landscape and to assist the public to enjoy beautiful countryside for the purpose of open air recreation.

It must be remembered, however, that although an area is designated a National Park, no additional rights of access are automatically bestowed on the visitor. Much of the land in the Northumberland National Park is privately owned, some by the Forestry Commission and some by the Ministry of Defence. So except where the National Park Authority makes special provision, the walker may only go by public rights of way, (i.e. minor roads, footpaths and bridleways) and even then, in the case of Ministry of Defence land, only when it is safe to do so. Red flags usually denote areas where it is forbidden and dangerous to enter for the time being.

A National Park Authority has a duty to conserve the landscape of its Park and to promote opportunities for people to enjoy it, but, in the latter case, only when due consideration has been given to the interests of those who live and work in the countryside. After all, it is the past care and attention by generations of landowners and farmers that has been largely responsible for the attractiveness of today's National Park landscape.

A National Park cannot become a rural museum. Farming and forestry practices go on changing, and if the countryside, as the farmers' and foresters' workshop, is to continue to make its valuable contribution to the Country's economy, then the landscape will go on changing and evolving too. However, the National Park Authorities are also planning authorities, and as such have some measure of control over what changes come about in the countryside.

Rights of way and using this booklet

Where hedges, walls and fences mark off land ownership or divide up individual farms, public rights of way make it possible to move across land, which is effectively the farmer's workplace, without interfering with his daily business of making a living from the land.

Apart from public roads (not necessarily 'made up') there are two types of right of way: footpaths and bridleways. Footpaths are simply routes which can be followed on foot, whilst bridleways, originally wide enough to accommodate a man leading a horse, may today be walked, or ridden on horseback or on pedal cycle.

As part of the programme involved in the production of this booklet all routes have been examined and signposts, stiles and waymarks provided where necessary. In some circumstances signposts or waymarks would be out of place. On such occasions, if the route is not obvious on the ground, greater detail is given in the notes and maps even to the extent of showing or explaining on which side of a hedge a path is located.

As far as possible maps are drawn with the minimum of fussiness; contour lines for example are omitted to avoid unnecessary visual confusion.

Interpretive notes are printed in the text in normal weight type, but to avoid confusion route directions are given in bold type whilst the letters '(R)' and '(L)' mean 'to the right' and 'to the left' respectively. Also, in the interests of clarity, only those rights of way which form the described routes are shown on the maps, which are all at 1:25000 (2½″ to the mile) scale.

The route symbols are as follows:

Footpath .... *Bridleway* — — — —
Permissive path —.—.— *Road* ————————

The terms 'footpath' and 'bridleway' indicate statutory rights of way and 'permissive path' indicates parts of the routes which walkers are permitted to use by courtesy of the landowner but which have no legal status.

Enjoy your walk

Comfort is essential to the enjoyment of any walks so wear comfortable sensible shoes or boots where a reading of the route notes might suggest it. Woollen socks, being more absorbent, are usually better to wear than those made from artificial fibres.

Walking may seem to be warm work but, especially at higher levels, it is possible to become chilled. Carry a pullover or jumper which can be put on if the temperature drops, and remember a waterproof will keep out the wind as well as keep off the rain.

A leisurely pace is a comfortable pace. Walks in this booklet have been calculated at roughly 1½ miles per hour to allow enough time for even the least experienced walker to complete the route.

Follow the Country Code

Guard against all risk of fire
Fasten all gates
Keep dogs under proper control
Keep to the paths across farm land
Avoid damaging fences, hedges and walls
Leave no litter
Safeguard water supplies
Protect wild life, wild plants and trees
Go carefully on country roads
Respect the life of the countryside.

Wooler

Wooler was one of the baronies into which Northumberland was divided after the Norman conquest. Henry I gave it to Robert de Muschampe on condition of his maintaining four knights fully equipped for the King's service. The castle, or tower, was built at an early date, for it is mentioned in 1254 as being a waste fortress of little value. Although it was rebuilt in the 16th century, all that remains today are a few blocks of masonry on a mound known as the 'Tory' above Church Street.

In the past there seems to have been some disrespect towards the Church, for records tell us that in 1313 John of Coldmartin struck a priest, and dressed in penitent's garb, was beaten three times round the parish church while the assembled townsfolk listened to a catalogue of his misdeeds. Later, in 1604, Rowland Scott was sued for drawing a dagger on John Jackson and appointing combat with him at the Communion table. But by the 18th century Wooler was quite a well-known health resort where invalids came to drink goats' whey.

Few famous people are associated with the town, although the celebrated Victorian wood engravers, the brothers Dalziel, who made many of the early blocks for 'Punch' were born in the town, and Josephine Butler, the Victorian social worker, died here in 1906. A plaque on a house front in Queen's Road commemorates the fact.

Despite having suffered severely from fire in 1693, 1722 and again in 1863, Wooler today is a thriving town with a shopping centre catering for many outlying hamlets and farms, as well as having a busy sheep and cattle market. Early closing day is Thursday. The Newcastle/ Edinburgh buses call at Wooler, and there is a regular service from Berwick and Alnwick. There are car parks and conveniences adjacent to the High Street.

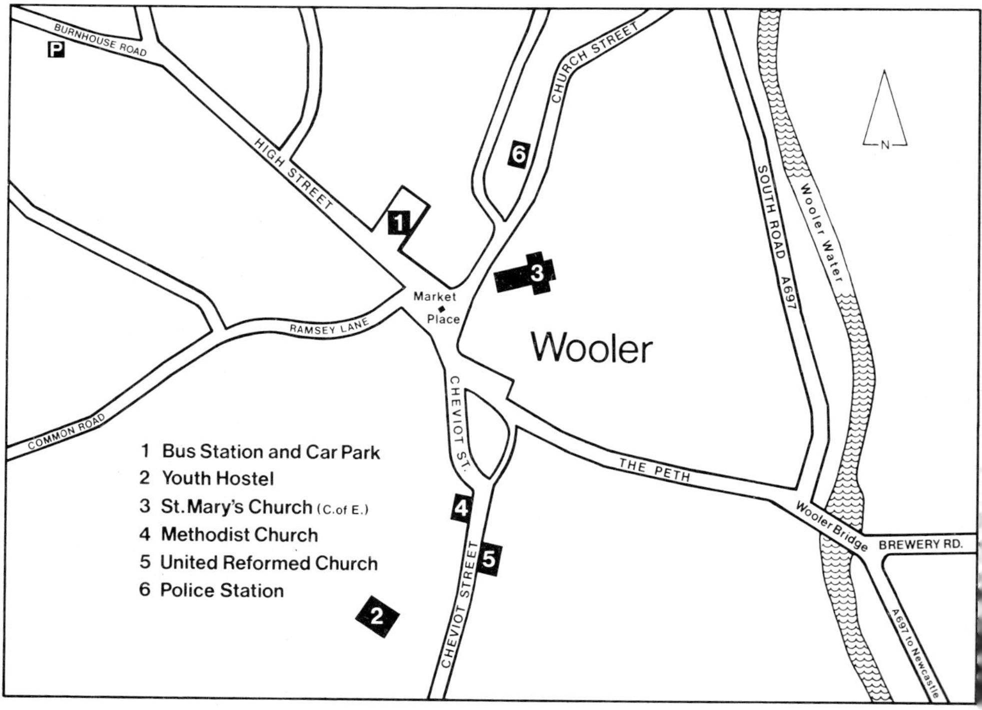

1 Wooler - Pin Well - Earle Mill; return via Carding Mill Plantation

3 miles, about 2 hours. Easy walking, no hills to climb, first on the outskirts of the town, then following a grassy way at the foot of the hills, returning along a country lane and a wooded path.

Walk up Cheviot Street at the southern end of Wooler High Street to the youth hostel. Take the footpath (R) at the side of the hostel driveway, leading to the junction of Ramsey Lane and Common Road. Turn left and walk a short distance along Common Road. Just before High Fair (R) is reached, go up the sloping track (L).

High Fair is named after the Fair which was held there in October during the late 19th century.

Walk along to the gate.

The cottage (L) is Waud House. In 1772 it belonged to the Greenwich Hospital Estates and was known as High Wade House, the rent being 3 guineas a year.

The path goes straight down the valley.

There are many deep dry channels in the Cheviots. They are thought to have been formed by melt-water flowing under pressure beneath the ice at the close of the last Ice Age, some 10,000 years ago.

The grassy hillside (L) is just the place for gorse (Ulex europaeus), also called furze or whin. In early summer this slope is a sheet of gold and the almond-scented yellow flowers perfume the air. Even in mid-winter, sheltered gorse bushes may bear flowers, giving rise to the old saying, 'When the gorse is not in flower, kissing is out of season'.

This is how a traction engine came to rest after running out of control down The Peth whilst towing trailers of a visiting circus in 1908.

Young gorse has soft, hairy leaves which are often grazed by sheep, giving the bush the appearance of a large ball. As the plant grows older, the new leaf material is produced as spines.

Broom (Sarothamnus scoparius) has a yellow flower and numerous, long erect branches, but no spines. It likes this dry, rather acid soil and, with gorse, is a food plant of the green hairstreak butterfly.

Follow the path down a slight slope.

The crag (R) is the King's Chair on which, according to legend, a king or chieftain once sat to watch the outcome of a battle. The small pool of water (R) fed by a spring, is the Pin Well. In olden days, on the 1st of May, a procession would form in Wooler and proceed to the Pin Well where maidens dropped bent pins into the water and made secret wishes. Superstition dies hard, for bent pins are still being cast into the water.

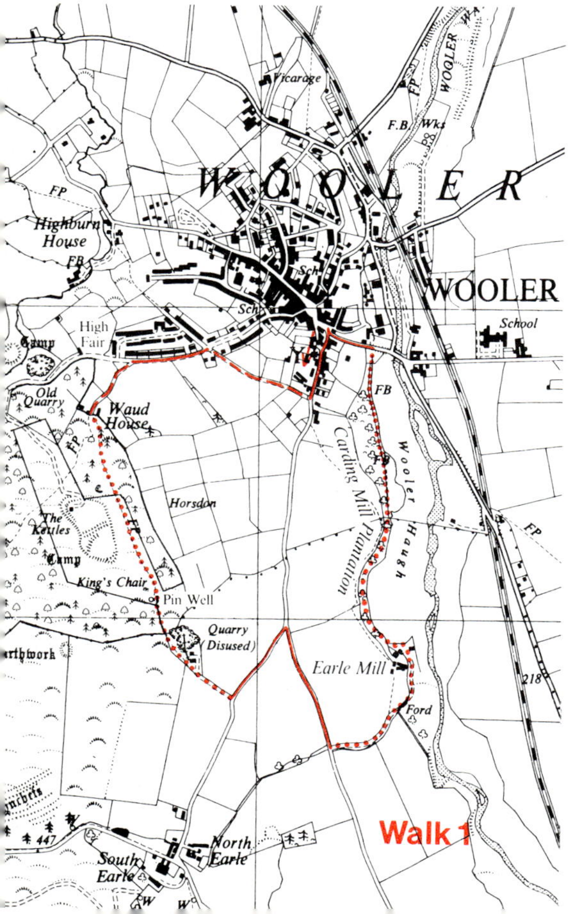

Pass through the gate ahead and walk to the road. Turn left and at the next junction turn right. Then take the first turning left to Earle Mill (L).

There is some lime in the soil here, so meadow cranesbill (Geranium pratense) brightens the foot of the lane (L) from June to September with its big, blue flowers.

The bare, waste ground was once part of a gravel extraction area. Weld (Reseda luteola) thrives in disturbed places; its tall spikes of yellow-green flowers are seen here in abundance in July and August.

Earle Mill is the site of a very old corn mill which was burned by the Scots in 1318 and again in the early 16th century. In 1663 a Mrs. Mary Selby was assessed at £20 for the tithes of the mill.

Walk around the building and, with the cottage garden gate and wall (L), follow the path through the trees and continue along the west side of the old mill race.

The small stream (R) is a leat which served Earle Mill, the Carding, Dye and Wooler Mills. A map of 1897 shows this water coming from a weir across Wooler Water and filling a pond immediately above Earle Mill. In a painting executed in 1885 the ruined Carding Mill (R) was shown as a three storey building. Carding wool is a process of teasing out clumps of wool fibres to run parallel to each other, thus preparing it for spinning. This was done by using wool cards: small boards to which were affixed pieces of cloth studded with little hooks. The tuft of wool was spread over one card and the other drawn across it until the wool was soft and fluffy. This mill was destroyed by fire in the early 20th century.

The path continues beside the old mill race straight to the road.

Across the road, down in the haulier's yard, is a red, pantiled building which was once a Dye Mill. A militia list of 1762 lists David Isaac and Andrew Corbett as dyers. Wooler Mill, dating back to the 13th century, was still in operation in 1925 and is now a building store at the foot of Church Street.

Turn left for the High Street.

2 Wooler-Weetwood Moor; return via Whitsunbank and Coldmartin Loughs

5 miles, about 3½ hours. A climb up on to a level moor with fine views all round, returning along an unmetalled road. Evening sunlight is best for viewing the sculptured rocks.

Cup and ring markings on Weetwood Moor

Walk down The Peth at the southern end of Wooler High Street. Cross the bridge and go along Brewery Road.

Glendale School (L) was built in 1953 on the site of a prisoner of war camp. The stone lions on the gate posts were made by the Italian prisoners.

Brewery Road takes its name from St. Magnus' Brewery which stood on a site by the farmhouse (L). The buildings, marked on a map of 1860, were pulled down in 1960 and the huge copper vats sold for a considerable sum. The cellars are under the farmyard and hops still grow in the hedge opposite.

Walk up the hill and where the road bends right, take the path (L) which leads to the gate and walk straight on for a few yards. Look for the sunken path (R) which leads up on to the moor. Take care not to follow any sheep track (L). Follow the cairns to the stile alongside the gate by the plantation (L).

The flat sculptured rocks lie a few yards to the left of the path near a stone cairn about 150 yards before the road is reached. The carvings are cup and ring markings, so called because each consists of a small hollow surrounded by a number of concentric rings. They date from about 1,600 BC, the time of the early Bronze Age.

The meaning of these symbols is obscure; possibly they were of religious significance. Bronze Age cists, burial boxes made from stone slabs, have been found with cup and ring markings on them.

Continue along the outcrop of rocks and on to the road.

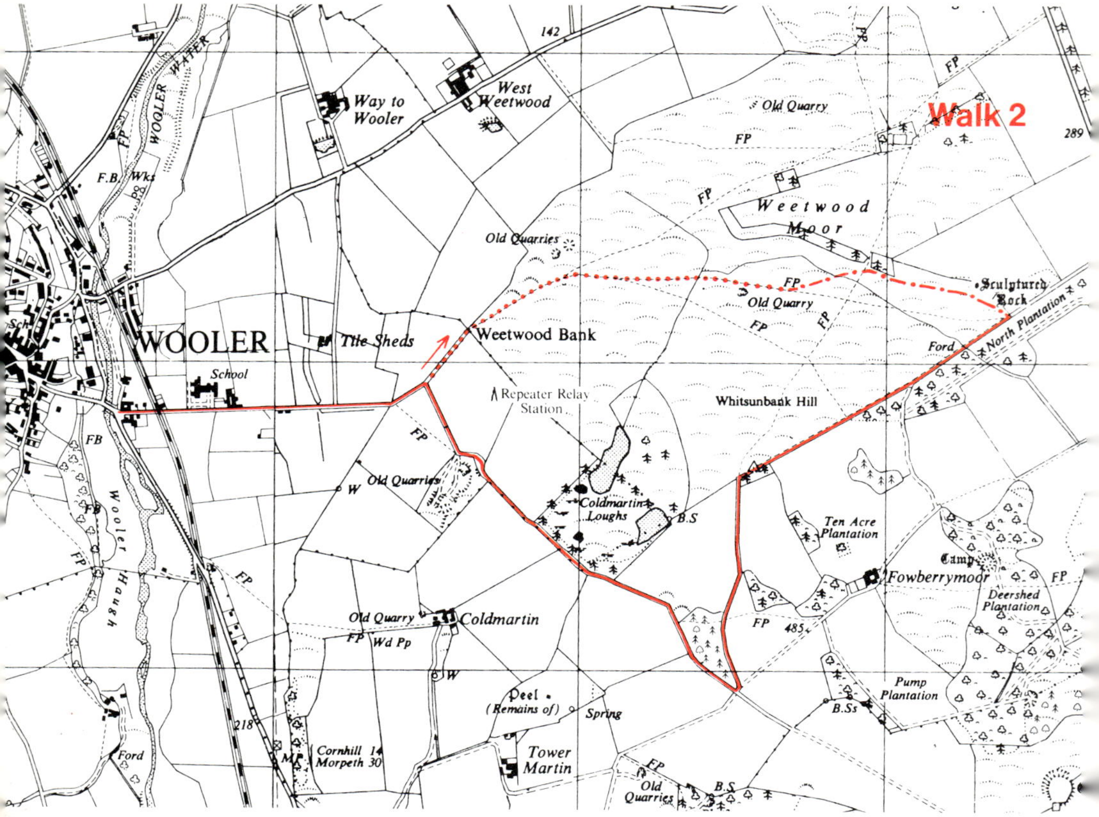

The damp moorland with its pools and swampy ground attracts red grouse and curlew. In the days of clan feuds the gutteral, barking call of the male grouse was rendered in Gaelic as 'co, co, mo chlaidh, mo chlaidh' (who, who, my sword, my sword). The curlew, Europe's largest wader, has a very long, down-curved bill with which it extracts worms and insects from the soft ground by the marshy pools.

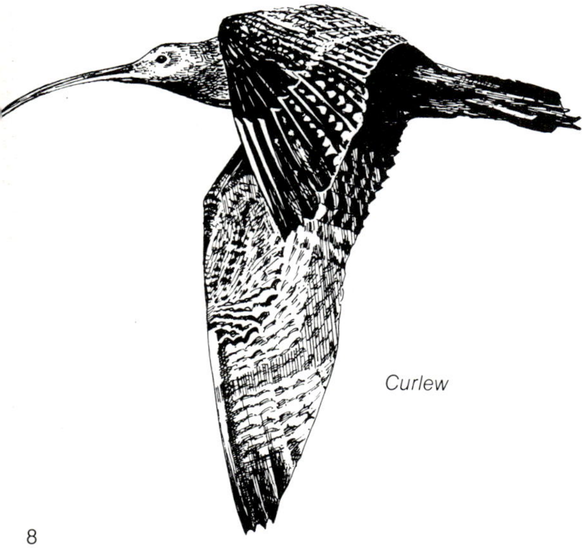

Curlew

This moor was once the site of the large, annual Whitsunbank Fair mentioned in 1595 when Sir John Carey, Governor of Berwick, reported to Queen Elizabeth I that Kerr of Cessford, a notorious Scottish landowner, had attended it. Kerr, at feud with the Storeys, had lain in wait between Akeld and Humbleton to ambush them and kill any folk on their way to the Fair. The Storeys had warning and escaped, so Kerr and his men went on to the Fair, to the consternation of the locals.

George Culley, the agriculturalist, in his book published in 1805, says the Fair was held on Whitsun Tuesday. It was certainly a big day; villagers came from miles around to buy at the stalls. Cattle, horses and sheep were sold, and servants were hired. Sir Walter Scott, the novelist, attended the Fair, and it is said that on one occasion he was entrusted with £30 of his shepherd's money to buy sheep, but he spent it on a horse instead. Whitsunbank Fair was discontinued in 1880.

At the road turn right and walk on to where the road is gated just beyond the trig point on the right.

The white painted triangulation pillar, or trig point (R), is used in survey work. The area to be surveyed is measured and mapped out by dividing it into triangles from a fixed point. These pillars are found on high land and are marked on maps as a triangle.

Pass through the gate and follow the track.

Coldmartin Loughs 'The Gull Ponds' (R) are gradually silting up. A peculiarity of these loughs is that even in the coldest weather they are never completely frozen. In the winter of 1548/9 a band of French and German mercenaries garrisoned at Jedburgh for the Scots, found on one of their forays into England, that the lough was one half frozen and one half free of ice.

The track turns sharp right and leads to a tarred road.

The Repeater Relay Station (R) was erected for the Post Office in the 1960's to relay very high frequency waves.

Follow the road down hill.

The sloping field (L) is a favourite haunt of oystercatchers. These large black and white wading birds, with a long orange bill, breed inland but move out to the coast during the autumn and winter.

Walk straight on for Wooler.

Local people gathering in the Market Place before travelling on to Wooler Fair. About 1900.

3 Wooler-Fowberry Moor Farm - Fowberry Mains; return via Weetwood Moor

6 miles, about 4 hours. A long climb out of Wooler with beautiful views of the Cheviots and Glendale. Passing through a farm yard, the walk continues in a plantation and along quiet country lanes, to return across the moor. A variation on previous walk.

Leave Wooler by The Peth, cross the bridge and walk along Brewery Road.

Follow the tarred road right up to the top of the hill and go along the unmetalled track.

The pretty cotton-grass (Eriophorum angustifolium) with its white, downy heads grows well in this wet, boggy area around Coldmartin Loughs (L).

At the point where the lane turns left, walk (L) a few steps, then cross the field to the farm buildings.

Fields like this, close to the farmstead, are called inbye land, as opposed to outbye, away from the farm. These fields are used at lambing time and for stock which the farmer wishes to keep under observation. ***The path leads right through Fowberry Moor Farm yard; please walk quietly and carefully.***

Dogs must be on a lead.

Walk (R) out of the farm yard and go through a gate straight ahead, beside the garages. Cross the fields to the plantation and walk through it.

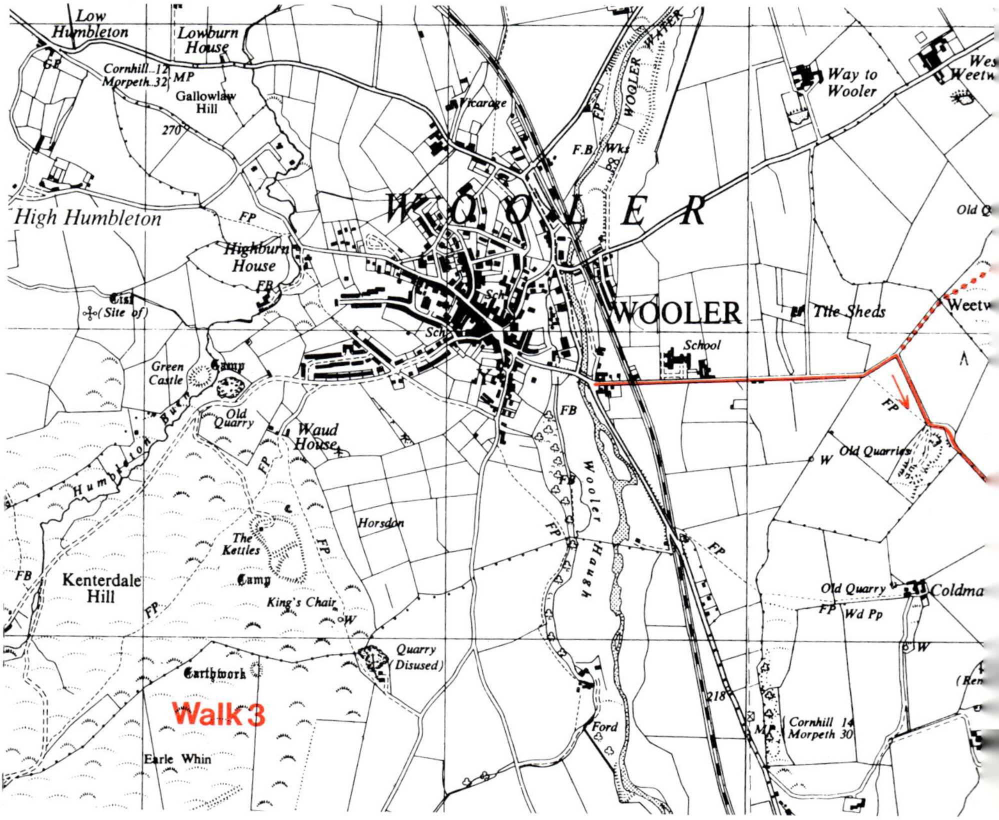

Cottongrass

This is Deershed Plantation, one of many scattered across the countryside which were planted to act as shelter-belts and to provide pheasant shooting.

This part of the plantation consists of coniferous trees planted so close together that they exclude the light; their fallen needles smother the ground, and the whole dark, woodland floor offers little encouragement to insects, birds and plants. The rhododendrons growing along this grassy ride indicate a shortage of lime in the soil.

They are not native British plants, but were widely introduced from the Himalayas in Victorian times.

Leave the plantation: pass just to the left of the cottage and walk (L) down the road.

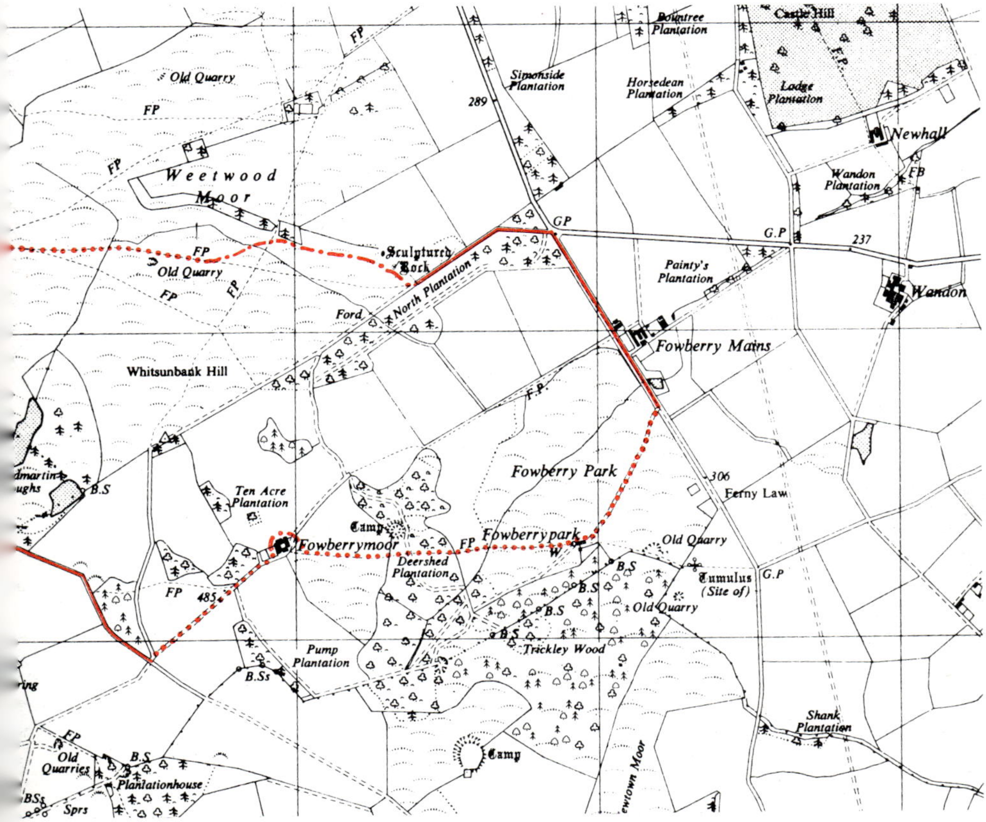

The line of hills (R) is the Fell Sandstone Ridge. It was formed some 300 million years ago, when large sandy deltas spread over most of the county. Later faulting and folding caused the steep, rocky escarpments which you can see, and which sweep in an arc from the Kyloe Hills, through Thrunton Crags to the Simonside Hills, with outcrops further westwards. The rock has been much quarried for its beautiful pink stone, used extensively in the Edinburgh district. Scattered all along the Fell Sandstone are rocks bearing cup and ring markings.

At the road turn left.

Fowberry Mains (R) was part of the estate in the possession of the Fowberry family during the reign of Edward I. In the 18th century it was owned and farmed by George Culley, the great agriculturalist, who developed the Border Leicester sheep from the Dishley breed.

Turn left at the crossroads.

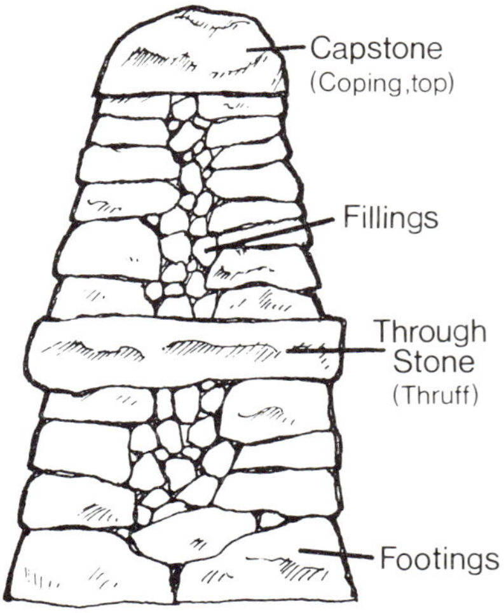

Section of dry-stone dyke

A few yards along the lane, look for the beech trees (L) with interlocking branches. The beautiful old walls are called dry-stone dykes, the building of which is a skilled craft, known to the Neolithic builders of chambered tombs and to people of the early Iron Age. Dry-stone dykes should never be clambered upon, because stones may be loosened and displaced, causing a serious weakness in the wall.

Just past the cattle grid, go through the gate (R), walk by the cairn and at the fence go over the stile by the plantation (R).

About 150 yards from the road, near a stone cairn, cup and ring markings can be clearly seen incised into one of the large flat rocks. These date from the early Bronze Age and their meaning is obscure.

Walk towards the next cairn (L) then with the plantation (R) continue straight across the moor.

Below lies Glendale, the valley of the River Glen which flows into the River Till, seen meandering across the flat expanse known as Milfield Plain. This area was scoured into a large hollow by ice during the Ice Ages, and later filled with melt-water to form a large lake which finally drained away through Etal Gorge some ten miles to the north-west. If you look behind the long roofs of Wooler Auction Mart at the right hand lower edge of the town, you will see one of the raised beaches of this lake. The tall chimney at Weetwood Farm just below was built at the time when threshing machines were steam driven. The long hill (R) with the shepherd's cottage near the summit, is Dod Law, and on the top is Wooler 9 hole golf course.

Walk down the slope, turn left at the bottom, and follow the path to the gate and on to the road and downhill for Wooler.

View of Cheviot Hills looking west from Weetwood Moor

Humbleton Burn Picnic Place

The Forestry Commission which owns about one fifth of the total area of the Northumberland National Park, laid out this picnic place in 1980. The road leads to Commonburn House, a remote farm, but half a mile on from the picnic place it becomes a bridleway and there is no public access by vehicle.

The distance from Wooler is a little over one mile; there is no bus service. Cars park on the grass just before the bridge.

4 Humbleton Burn Picnic Place - Browns Law; return via Wooler Common Farm

2½ miles, about 1¾ hours. A short climb uphill, then an easy, pleasant walk on good paths along the lower slopes of the hills.

Leave Wooler by Ramsey Lane and follow Common Road to the picnic place. Cross the bridge and take the footpath (R) beside the burn.

Monkey flower (Mimulus guttatus), a yellow flower with red blotches, grows here because it likes wet places by shallow streams.

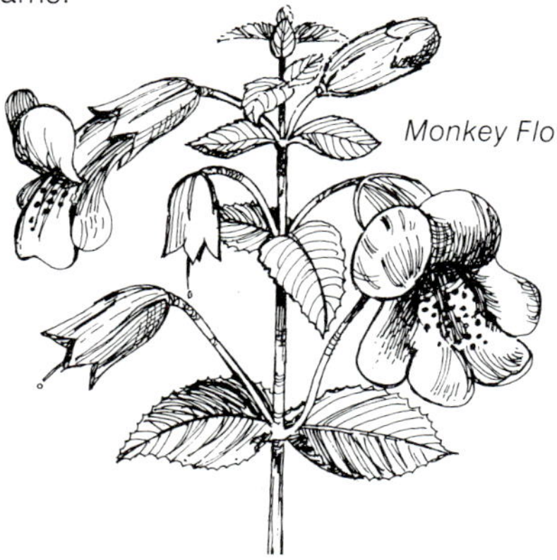

Monkey Flower

As the path starts to climb the hill, notice the rectangular depression in the ground (L). In the First World War the militia used to come up here and practise rifle shooting. The targets were hoisted from behind the nearer ridge; the soldiers down the valley shot at them, and the bullets buried themselves harmlessly in the second, larger ridge. In old guide books this area is always called 'The Targets'.

Harebells (Campanula rotundifolia), heath bedstraw (Galium saxatile) and lady's bedstraw (Galium verum) all prefer dry, grassy places, so this path is an ideal spot for them.

Go through the gate and walk straight on.

Cheviot sheep graze here. In bygone times they were known as the 'Long Breed'; today they are shorter and more compact than the earlier type. The sheep are white-faced, hornless, and generally dip in the back. This breed is best suited to lower upland grazings. Mated with a Border Leicester ram, the Cheviot ewes produce Scots half-bred lambs. The Border Leicester stands high off the ground; it has a white face with a Roman nose, no horns, long ears which lie forward, and ragged wool.

Whinchats favour this area. They perch on top of the bracken. Notice the white eye stripe. At the end of summer the whinchats leave for their winter quarters around the Mediterranean or in Africa.

Pass through the next gate and turn left.

The sunken parallel tracks (R) were probably made by cattle being driven across the hill in days gone by.

Follow the fence (L) to the gate and then walk downhill, through the gorse, just below the line of trees (R). Turn left at the road and follow it for a short distance before walking down the broad, grassy track to the burn (R).

This is part of a local drove road once used to drive cattle to summer grazing grounds or to market. The width of the track allowed for grazing en route. In some places these old drove roads were called 'streets': Clennel Street and The Street cross the Cheviot Hills from the Upper Coquet to Scotland.

Go through the gate and follow the path up the right hand lower slopes of the hill to pass Wooler Common Farm (R).

Hay baling at Wooler Common Farm

Wooler Common, where the townsfolk had rights of pasturage, was enclosed in 1867 and nine freeholders obtained allotments of less than one acre each.

Pass the farmhouse and walk to the left, around the low hill. A clear track leads down to a stile and on to the picnic place.

Border Leicester

Cheviot

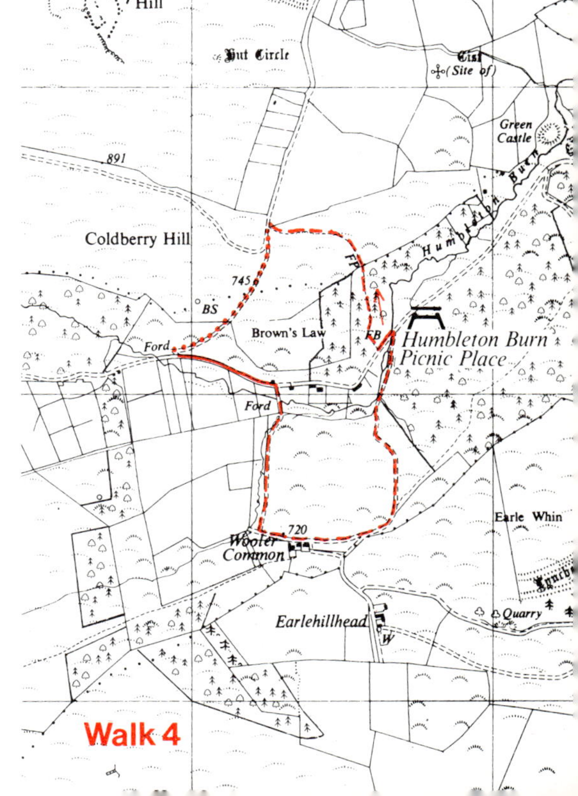

5 Humbleton Burn Picnic Place - Hellpath; return via Commonburn House

7 miles, about 4½ hours. This walk, with no hills to climb, takes one right into Cheviot country. The return route, along a couple of miles of unfenced, metalled bridleway, offers fine views. Walking boots advisable.

Leave Wooler by Ramsey Lane and follow Common Road to the picnic place. Just before the bridge take the footpath (L) beside the burn, cross the stile and follow the track which turns left and passes around the low hill (R) and close by Wooler Common Farm (L). At the wall end (L) just past the building, go through the gate, cross the field and follow the clear path straight on by the plantation (L) and cross the moor.

The Curlew, emblem of the Northumberland National Park, breeds on these upland moors. Its hauntingly beautiful call, 'courlee', is the very essence of the National Park. Its bubbling song, usually produced during a gliding flight, can be heard during the breeding season. Merlin, our smallest falcon, hunt over the open hilly moorland which offers fences and stones upon which they like to perch. They feed on small birds – often pipits – that are pursued and caught in mid air.

Watch Hill (R) with its craggy summit, was one of the many places where lookouts were posted during the turbulent days of the Border troubles in the 15th and 16th centuries.

Wheatear

The path leads straight on to a stile – a detour (R) will avoid the boggy patch – and Hellpath.

This name may be a corruption of Hill path.

Hartheugh with its glidders (L) towers above Carey Burn as it flows on to join the Harthope.

Every spring the wheatears return to the glidders of Hartheugh (L) and many other places on these open hills, from their winter quarters in Africa. Their pure white rump is very noticeable as they flit about close to the ground.

Cross the fence at the bottom of Hellpath, turn right and walk to the confluence of the burns. Cross the water and take the path up the slope and follow it for a while until a few yards from the gate.

View from Hellpath of Carey Burn below Watch Hill

One day every year in early summer, this path is alive with running figures. The Youth Hostels Association organises Chevy Chase, a race from Wooler to the top of The Cheviot, Hedgehope and Langlee Crags, and back by the road. There are three groups, juniors who run only to the top of The Cheviot; seniors, often quite elderly, who walk the route; and harriers, representing nation-wide clubs, who run all 17 miles of this gruelling course. There are check points at the ruins of Broadstruther seen ahead, on The Cheviot, where the Mountain Rescue Team mans a first aid tent and on Hedgehope and Langlee Crags. Usually about 200 people take part, and very few fail to complete the Chase.

Just before the gate is reached, turn right and walk a short distance uphill towards the large, upstanding stone. Notice the red shed (R) with a low hill to the left of it. Walk to the left of that hill and go through the gate near the foot of the crags, continuing on in the direction of the house. At the next fence turn right, follow it, and go through the gate just past the

The valley of the Carey Burn

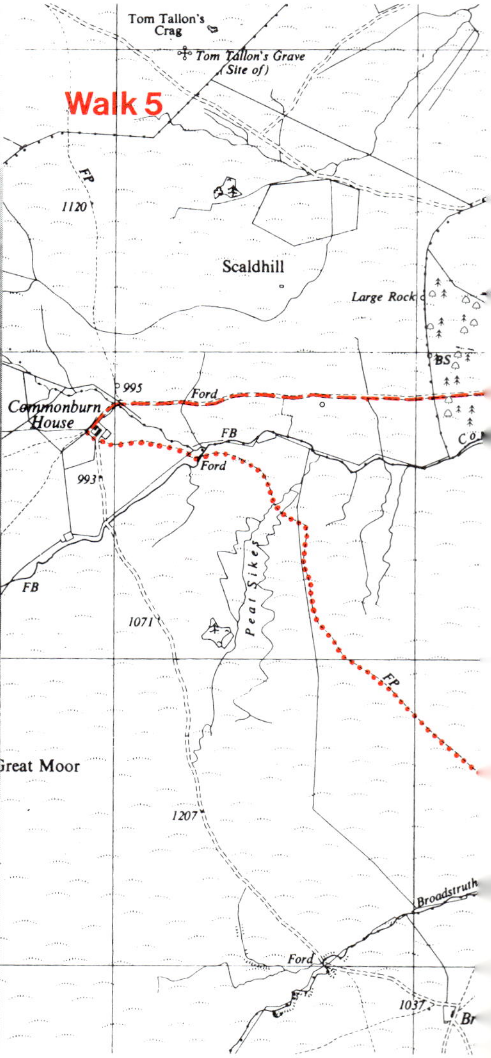

stell. Walk towards the house (Commonburn House).

Commonburn House – a shepherd's cottage – stands at a height of almost 1,000 feet.

Cross the burn and walk straight on to the gate by the farmyard (L).

Please walk quietly and quickly across this pasture close to the house, called inbye land. Dogs must be on a lead.

Turn right at the road.

About a mile and a half from Commonburn House the lone cottage of Bell's Valley (L) set back from the road, stands near a series of trough-like dry valleys called The Trows. These are glacial meltwater channels, carved out by water flowing under pressure beneath the ice, towards the end of the Ice Age, some 10,000 years ago.

The plantations, mostly of spruce which gives them a dark forbidding look, are owned by the Forestry Commission. A short distance further on, the sheltered gorse-clad slope opposite Browns Law Farm (R) is a favourite haunt of yellowhammers.

Follow the road back to the picnic place.

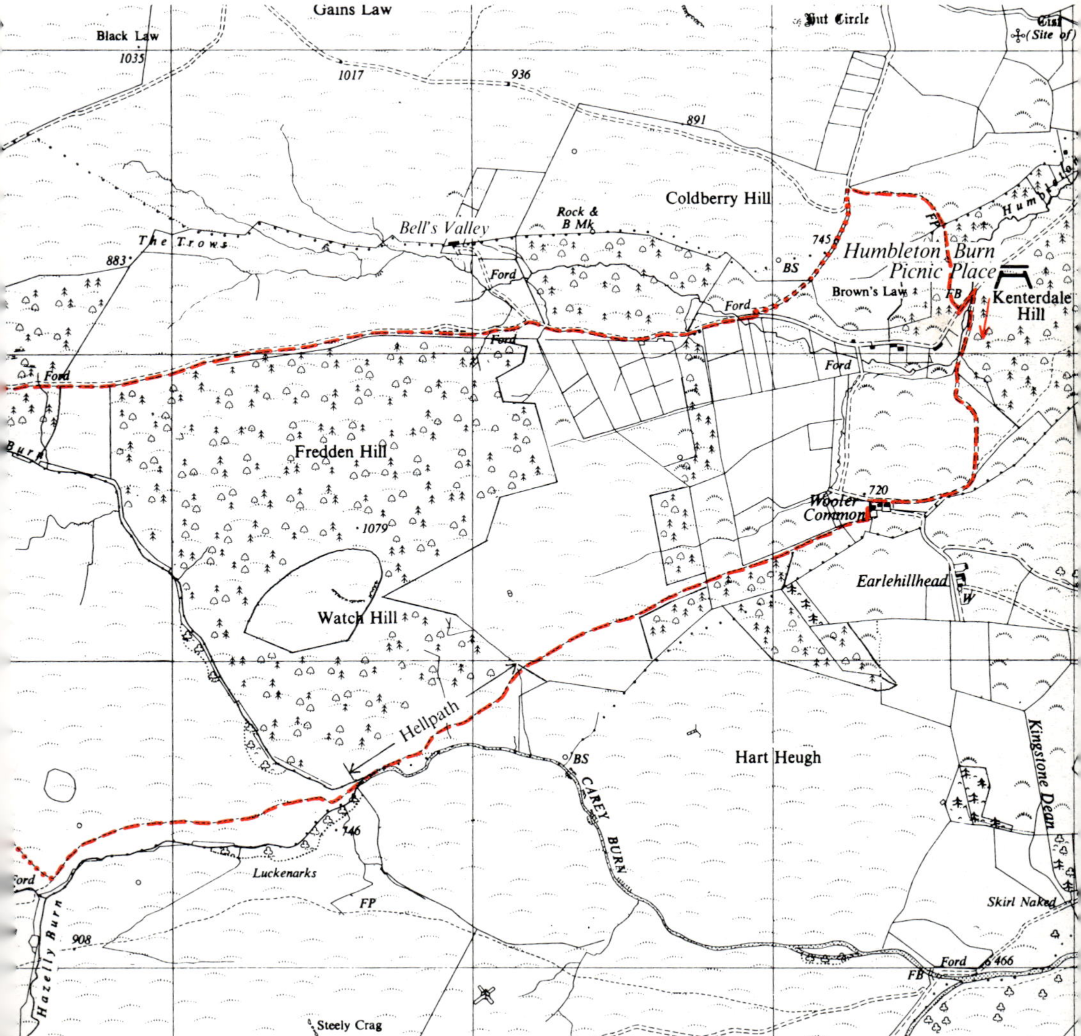

High Humbleton

Today High Humbleton is a tiny hamlet, but many years ago it was a fair-sized village. In the Lay Subsidy Rolls of 1296 it was assessed for tax purposes at £39, which was a large sum in those days. However, in 1580 the village was too small to have any tenant of sufficient substance to maintain a horse and armour for the defence of the Border.

There was a church and churchyard and a number of cottages clustered around the village green. In the 19th century the gravestones were broken up by the local housewives into sand-stones for cleaning hearths and floors. The later decline of the village was no doubt caused by the absorption of small freeholdings by large landowners.

The common lands between Humbleton and Akeld were enclosed in 1867 and a small piece of common land between Humbleton and Wooler was enclosed in 1869, when nine freeholders obtained allotments of less than one acre each.

High Humbleton is about one mile from Wooler via Burnhouse Road. There is no bus service. Turn left at the telephone kiosk at the hamlet; cars may park on the grass where the tarred road ends, just past the ruined cottage. If you are approaching from the A697 go up the hill at Low Humbleton and straight on.

6 High Humbleton - Coldberry Hill; return via Humbleton Hill

3 miles, about 2 hours. A fairly gentle climb on a good path to nearly 1,000 feet with wide views. Return by the lower slopes of an historic hill.

Looking north across Milfield Plain

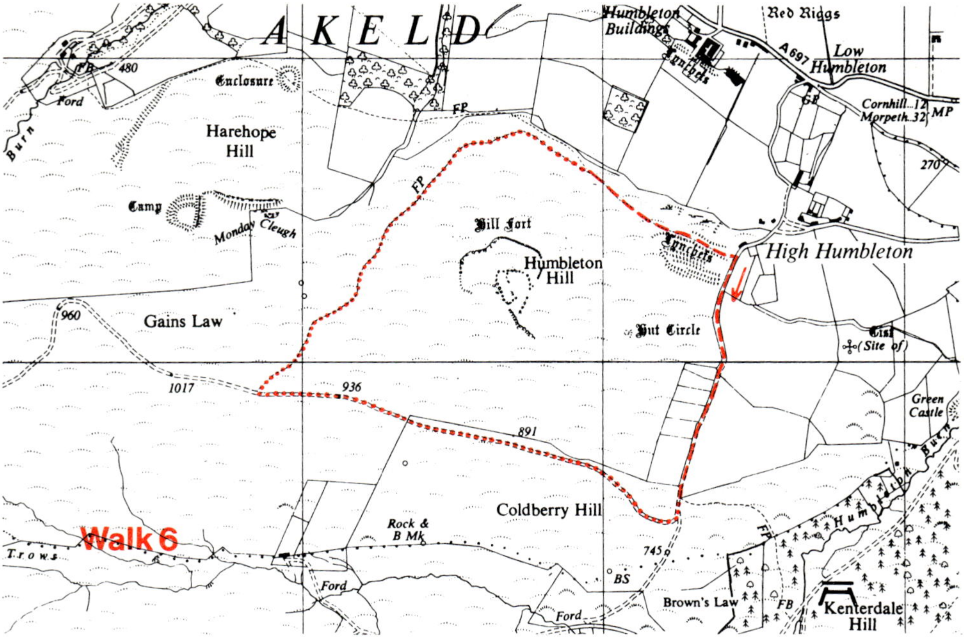

From the parking space where the tarred road ends, walk along the lane and up the slope for about 400 yards to the gate.

The enclosure with its tumbled stones to the right of the gate is all that remains of a cottage called Drythropple (dry throat), possibly because it lacked water.

A few yards past the gate turn right and follow the path uphill.

The pretty little yellow flower, tormentil (Potentilla erecta) is to be found in many places on the Cheviots. It thrives in heathy, grassy areas where the soil is acidic.

On Humbleton Hill (R) was a prehistoric hill fort. The summit is still partially encircled by the tumbled walls of the stout stone rampart which protected a citadel-like enclosure. There are many such forts and related settlements scattered across the Cheviots. They date from the Bronze Age, some 2½ thousand years ago, and were in use perhaps right up to and beyond the time of the Roman occupation.

Follow the path, pass through the gap in the wall and walk on for a few hundred yards, turning right by the small cairn. A clear path is soon found, leading downhill along the lower slopes of Humbleton Hill.

The rocky cleft in Harehope Hill (L) is Monday Cleugh. This dry valley is considered to be a sub-glacial spillway, eroded by meltwater flowing under pressure beneath the ice towards the end of the last Ice Age.

Notice at the head of the cleugh the ramparts of a prehistoric promontory fort.

Tormentil

On the 13th of September 1402 this area was the scene of a battle. The Scots under Douglas were returning from a raid in Northumberland, when they were intercepted by the Earl of Northumberland and his son, Harry Hotspur, with a force of English archers. The archers, in Monday Cleugh, shot up hill at the Scots on the slopes of Humbleton Hill and, according to a chronicler of the time, the devastating shower of arrows made the Scots look like hedgehogs. The English won the day. A field across the A697 at the bottom of Humbleton Hill, is called Red Riggs because it was the scene of severe fighting. Many human skulls and bones of horses have been ploughed up there. News of this battle forms the start of Shakespeare's play 'Henry IV'.

Near the foot of the hill the path turns right, then runs beside a wall (L) and a pond (L).

Just past the pond, on the slope (R) are lynchets. These are low banks marking the outlines of early ploughing. Lynchets are often difficult to date, but most are Anglo Saxon or medieval. Early 19th century cultivation terraces in Northumberland, on poor land, can resemble much older lynchets.

The gate to the lane at High Humbleton is a few yards ahead.

7 High Humbleton - Gleadscleugh; return via Black Law and Gains Law

6 miles, about 4 hours. Choose a fine, clear day for this walk, to enjoy the wide views and spaciousness of the hills. Good paths with one short, rough patch, and no very steep hills to climb. Walking boots are advisable.

Go through the gate by the ruin (R) where the tarred road ends: walk slightly to the right to pick up the grassy path by the marshy ground and on beside the pond (R).

The sike has been dammed to create this duck-shooting pond. The hides are seen at the edge.

With the wall (R) follow the path and step across the sike to reach a gate just to the left of the small wood seen ahead.

The bracken grows quite tall in the summer, and can be a nuisance. Cattle help to kill it by trampling, but in early autumn it is poisonous to them and they have to be removed from it. Spraying has proved very expensive and not entirely satisfactory. In the back end, as autumn is called in Northumberland, the hills are a glory of yellow and red, as the bracken turns colour before dying down.

Go through the gate and straight up the slope.

This grassy slope has been 'improved' and cleared of bracken, but left undisturbed for some time now, so the wild flowers have been able to re-establish themselves.

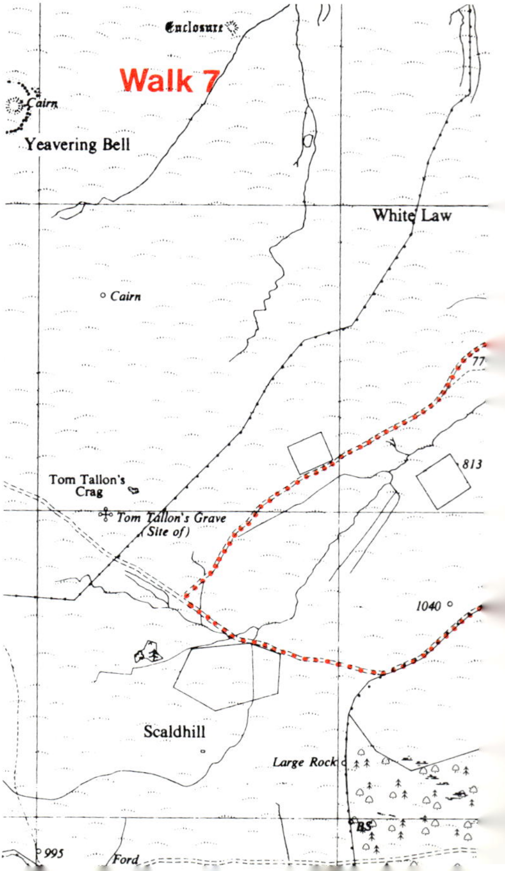

Pass through the next gate and along the lower slopes of Harehope Hill.

The cluster of red-roofed buildings (R) is Bendor. A couple of fields to the right of them, by the road, may be seen, if not obscured by a standing crop, a large stone. This is probably prehistoric, but is marked on maps as the site of the Battle of Homildon, or Humbleton, Hill 1402.

The big house in the park is Ewart. Count Horace St. Paul, who served in the Austrian army in the 18th century, built the house and laid out the park, creating a model estate.

Away to the left of Ewart is a ridge of low hills crowned with clumps of trees. Behind that ridge was fought the battle of Flodden Field in 1513, when the English army completely routed the Scots. A monument has been erected on the spot, and a remembrance service is held there each year.

The path leads down the slope to a wall (R).

The hamlet of Akeld is seen below. The 1296 Lay Subsidy Roll showed the 'township' of

Gate on the approach to Harehope Hill

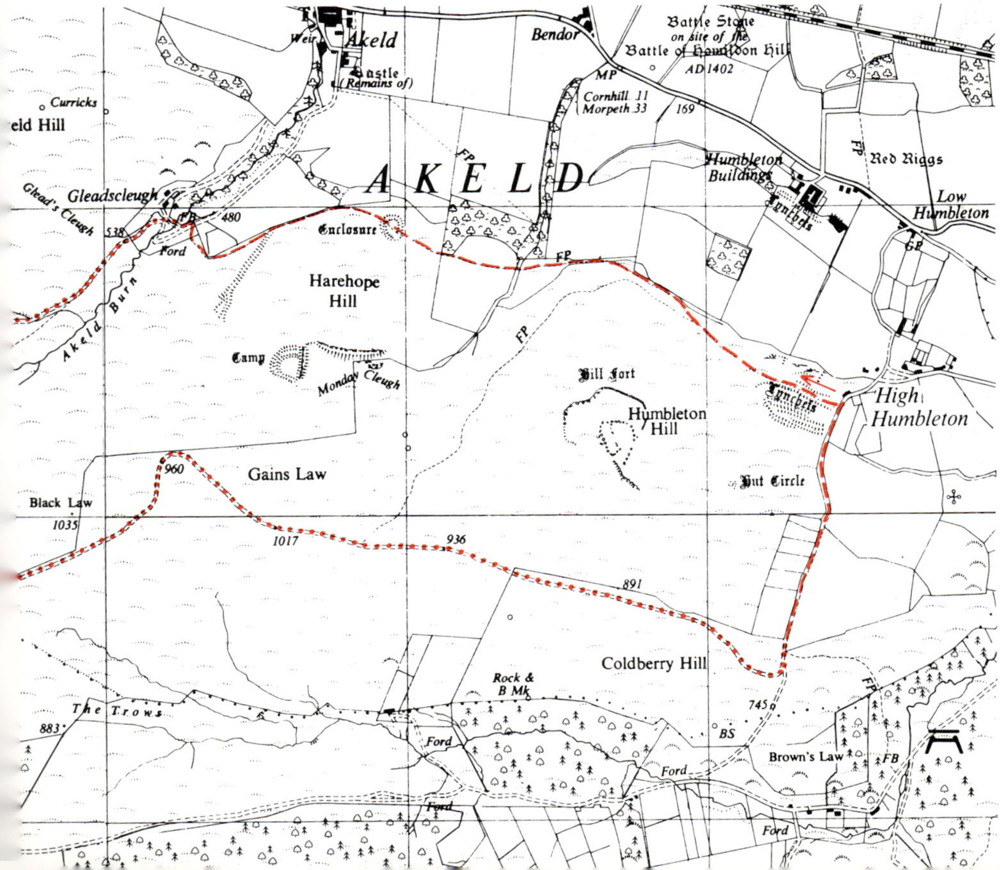

Akeld to be prosperous and wealthy, since the movables of the 13 householders reached the sum of £53. Notice the stone building standing on its own near the foot of the hill. This is a bastle house. It was mentioned in 1522 when Lord Dacre proposed to place ten men there, under John Wallis, for the protection of the Border. In times of raid, cattle would have been driven into the tunnel-vaulted ground floor, while the townsfolk took refuge upstairs. In a Border Survey of 1541 the bastle was mentioned as a 'lytle fortelett or castle house'.

Follow the wall as it turns abruptly right, walk downhill, bear left near the bottom, cross the burn by the little bridge and go up the slope.

Gleadscleugh was once a pair of shepherds' cottages. Today many of these isolated cottages are used as holiday homes, or allowed to fall into disrepair. The cleugh is the gully to the left of the cottage.

Turn left and follow the path above Akeld Burn. After about half a mile the clear path is lost in rougher ground, but walk to within a few hundred yards of the clump of trees seen ahead. At the cairn turn left and walk towards the gate in the wall a little distance to the left of the plantation. The rough ground extends only to the gate.

This short stretch of rough walking gives some idea of what most of the Cheviot moors were like before drainage was undertaken. In fact, some parts of this large, hill-encircled basin, especially around Commonburn House (R), were quite dangerous at one time.

The common sundew (Drosera rotundifolia) likes this type of ground.

Roe deer breed in the plantations and roam the hills. Small shy creatures, they are usually seen bounding away across the hills, jumping the fences with effortless ease. Roe deer have only a rudimentary tail, and the conspicuous rump patch called the 'target' is yellowish or even orange in summer, and white in winter.

Do not go through the gate but turn left, beside the wall (R).

A glance back discloses Yeavering Bell (R) with its tumbled stone ramparts which enclosed the largest Iron Age hill fort in Northumberland. To the left of it is Tom Tallon's Crag. Nothing is known of an individual of that name, and it is perhaps derived from the Celtic 'tomen' tumulus, 'tal' forehead or promontory, 'llan' enclosure. Many years ago a huge cairn covering a cist with bones stood near the crag, but it was robbed to build the stone dykes.

The long hill with the rock like a point at one end, is Wester Tor. On the other side of it lies the College Valley.

Go through the gate at the junction of the wall and the wire fence. Walk on and through the next gate, with the wall now on your left. Where this wall turns left, walk straight on, following the tractor route which curves round (L) to meet a wall. Go through the gate (R) to pick up the clear path running just below the summit of Gains Law.

Pause a moment to look back at Black Law. An archaeological dig in the summer of 1980 showed that the circular patches of bracken among the heather were the sites of Bronze Age huts. A burial ground on the summit of Gains Law, excavated at the same time, disclosed a cist with bones and pottery, thought to be connected with the settlement which was in existence some 3½ thousand years ago.

Common sundew

View west from Harehope Hill with Yeavering Bell on the skyline

Follow the path as it runs gently downhill.

These hills were formed from the outpourings of lava from the Cheviot volcanoes which were in eruption about 380 million years ago. The lava cooled and hardened into a rock called Andesite.

Later intrusions of molten material into the lava hardened into 'dykes' of a more acid rock which forms a soil upon which heather will grow. The heather is burnt every three or four years to encourage new shoots for sheep grazing. Areas of heather are called Black Lands.

This heather clad moorland is a hunting ground for the short-eared owl (the 'ears' are very short feathery tufts). It flies during the day rather than at night, and feeds on short-tailed voles. Numbers increase dramatically in Britain when vole populations crash in Scandinavia, as birds cross the North Sea.

Snipe, too, favour this type of ground, nesting in coarse grass or rushes. During display flight, a vibrating, bleating sound is produced by the widely spread outer tail feathers.

At the bottom of the hill turn left, go through the gate and walk down the lane to High Humbleton.

The Harthope Valley

This beautiful valley is one of several which run deep into the heart of the Cheviot Hills. It was formed by geological faulting and scoured out by ice spilling down from the top of The Cheviot during the Ice Age.

The Harthope Burn has its source on the slopes of The Cheviot.

The single track roads in these valleys lead only to isolated farms; most are private roads, some are bridleways.

There are many sheep in the valley so drive carefully and keep dogs on a lead.

There is no public transport to the Harthope; cars may park on grassy spaces by the roadside.

8 Harthope Valley - Langlee - Old Middleton; return above Happy Valley

4½ miles, about 3 hours. A climb on a good path to a hill giving a fine view of the Harthope Valley. Easy walking over the hill; good views eastward; returning above the Happy Valley.

Cars park on the grassy space (R) just before the first bridge in the valley. Walk over the bridge.

The kestrel, sometimes called the windhover because of its habit of apparently hanging motionless in the air, patrols the hillsides. From a considerable height its keen eyes detect the movement of mice, beetles and other small creatures.

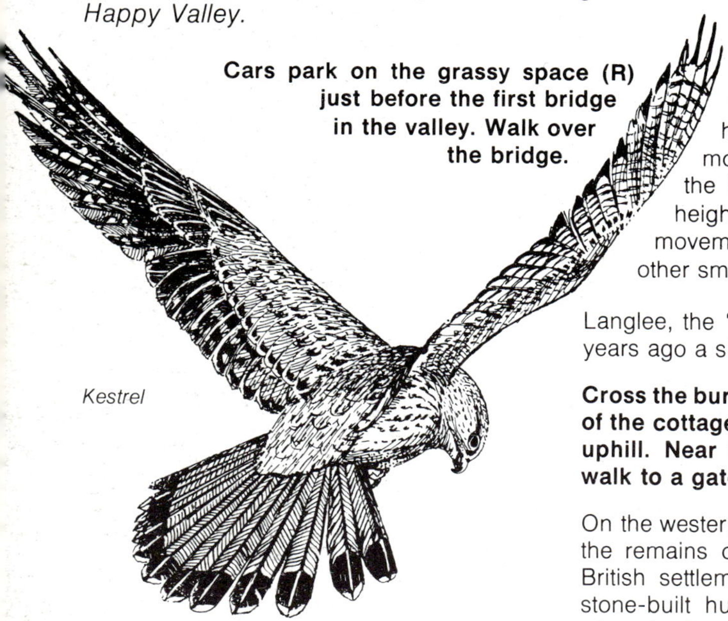

Kestrel

Carey Burn bridge was built in 1956. Prior to this there was a wooden bridge and a small stone footbridge, but they were both washed away in the floods of 1948. Only the abutments of the old stone bridge remain.

Continue along the road about one mile to the cottage (L).

Brown trout swim in the Harthope Burn, providing food for herons which fish the water. These birds stand hunched and motionless a long time, watching and waiting to pounce.

Langlee, the 'long clearing' was until a few years ago a shepherd's cottage.

Cross the burn by the bridge, pass in front of the cottage garden and follow the path uphill. Near the top, cross a track and walk to a gate seen on the skyline.

On the western slopes of Brands Hill (L) are the remains of at least a dozen Romano-British settlements which contained round stone-built huts. They are difficult to see when the bracken is high.

Go through the gate and follow the grassy path which bears a little to the left and goes downhill to a fence. Step over the ladder stile and walk across the field with the fence (R). Cross the next stile: the fence is now (L) and pass in front of the cottage.

The Harthope Burn near Langlee

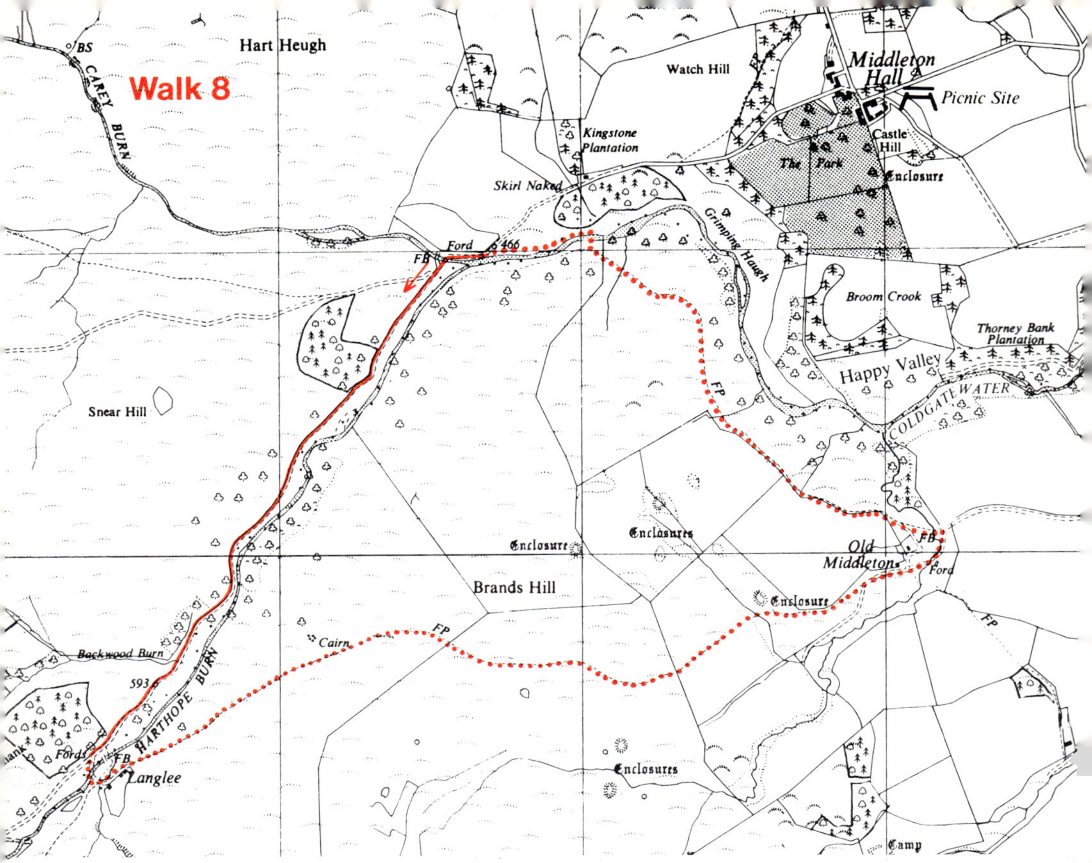

The shepherd's cottage is all that remains of Old Middleton, or Middleton Old Town. The foundations of other buildings can be seen (R). In medieval times a village consisted of the Lord of the Manor, two or three free tenants, a few dozen villein farmers and about half a dozen cottagers. Most of the population lived on isolated farms or in a township (Old English 'tun' - a homestead). These townships were divided into farms of 30 or so acres. They were self-sufficient, having their own bakery and tannery and use of the Lord's mill. Spinning and weaving were done at home. The right of turbary entitled them to cut turf from the common pit, and this provided a roofing material. Round the town would be three or four Town Fields, sown with barley, beans or wheat, and fallowed in rotation.

This town was called 'Old Middleton' on old maps.

In 1810 James Rea leased North Middleton at a rental of £1,350 and a clause in the deeds stated that a barn for a threshing machine was to be built at the Old Town.

Follow the track around a little slope and, near the wall, turn left and cross the bridge. Cross the field near the fence (R): go over the stile and walk beside the plantation and on above the valley.

This is the Happy Valley, and here the Harthope Burn which was crossed at Langlee is called Coldgate Water.

At the gate walk along the top of the slope with the fence to your right. Continue above the pond to the stile, then walk downhill bearing left. Cross a second stile beyond the gap in the wall and follow the track to the footbridge.

The old trees by the bridge are encrusted with lichens which grow well here in the clean atmosphere. Many do not tolerate pollution and will not survive near smoky towns.

Turn left after crossing the bridge and return to the main road and the starting point.

9 Harthope Valley - Lambden Valley - Broadstruther; return via Rushy Gair and Hawsen Burn

5½ miles, about 3½ hours. A walk, rough in places, into the heart of the hills. No steep climbs. Choose a fine, clear day as landmarks are few. Walking boots advisable.

Follow the Harthope Valley road to a point about half a mile past the lone cottage of Langlee (L). Cars may park on the grassy space beside the road (L). Take the bridleway (R), signposted 'Broadstruther, Wooler Common', up the hill. The path runs above the road, but just before the stell is reached, it turns right, above the Hawsen Burn.

Stells are circular enclosures of stone used for sheltering sheep. They are of various types; some are divided into several 'rooms'; some have a projecting wall to provide added shelter; some are backed against mountain walls, but most are free-standing and often in remote places. In south-east Scotland they are called 'bields'; in west Scotland 'fanks'.

The farm of Langleeford can be seen through the trees (L). It was mentioned in 1552 in connection with night watches for marauding Scots. In 1791 Sir Walter Scott is said to have spent a happy holiday at the farmhouse, enjoying the fishing, the walking and the sight of the pretty dairy-maid who brought him goat's whey to drink every morning.

Follow the path towards another stell seen ahead.

A typical stell

Pause a moment and look back at the big crag of Housey seen across the valley. Some 380 million years ago this area was subjected to intense volcanic activity, beginning with outbursts of great explosive violence. This was followed by lava flows, and the sequence continued for a long period of time. Later a great dome of magma (molten rock) welled up beneath the volcanoes of The Cheviot and Hedgehope, cooling at depth to form granite. Where this molten mass met the lava its intense heat changed it chemically into a different, harder type of rock. Thus we have the Metamorphic Aureole, or ring of changed rock, around The Cheviot (known locally as simple 'Cheviot'). Gradual wearing away of the surface exposed the harder rock which is visible in places as upstanding, block-like tors. Much later, during the time of the Ice Ages local ice sheets from the Cheviot massif flowed across the higher ground, sheering these tors. Housey Crag and Langlee Crags across the valley, are streamlined north to south – the direction of the ice movement.

Walk almost to the head of the burn then bear slightly right continuing up the heather-covered slope to the fence;

Harthope Valley from above the Hawsen Burn with Housey Crag prominent in the centre

Broadhope Hill appearing (R). Go over the stile in the fence.

The Cheviot (L) at 2,676 feet (815 m) is the highest hill in the range. Its flat summit is one vast peat bog. Rainwater cannot sink into the granite rock, so heather, moss and grasses do not decompose properly, and form the thick covering of black peat. The presence of granite which makes for a more acid soil encourages the growth of heather, or ling (Calluna vulgaris). Where the moor is wet and boggy one finds cross-leaved heath (Erica tetralix), a most attractive plant with its little clump of pink flowers at the tip of the stem.

Cross-leaved heath

In 1728 Daniel Defoe ascended The Cheviot on horseback, much afraid that he would find the summit a knife-edged ridge. The local boys who accompanied him laughed at this, assuring him that an army could stand upon the top.

Walk straight ahead to the stone cairn, then towards the lower edge of the plantation seen ahead on the right hand side of the valley.

The remote Lambden Valley, with only a few shepherds' cottages scattered along its length, leads into the College Valley.

On reaching the plantation go over the stile alongside the wide gate and walk along the forestry road for about 150 yards to where the road bends. Bear right up the grass track through the plantings to the stile in the fence.

The blackfaced sheep on these uplands are 'hefted' on to the land, which means that if the farm is sold, the sheep remain. Born and bred for generations on certain hillsides, the sheep gain an immunity to the diseases carried on the land; they know where to find shelter from the wind and where the best spring 'bite' is to be found. Each year some ewe lambs are retained by the farmer to replace older beasts.

Cross the stile keeping the fence on your right. After a while cross this fence via another stile and look for a cairn marking the route on the slope ahead. Follow the narrow path towards the distant trees of ruined Broadstruther Farm. About 100 yards from another fence turn right and follow the path around the slope, the domed summit of Hedgehope Hill coming into view.

The sheep farmers and their shepherds patrol these hills on horseback, in a Land-rover or, latterly, on a scrambler bike. Their

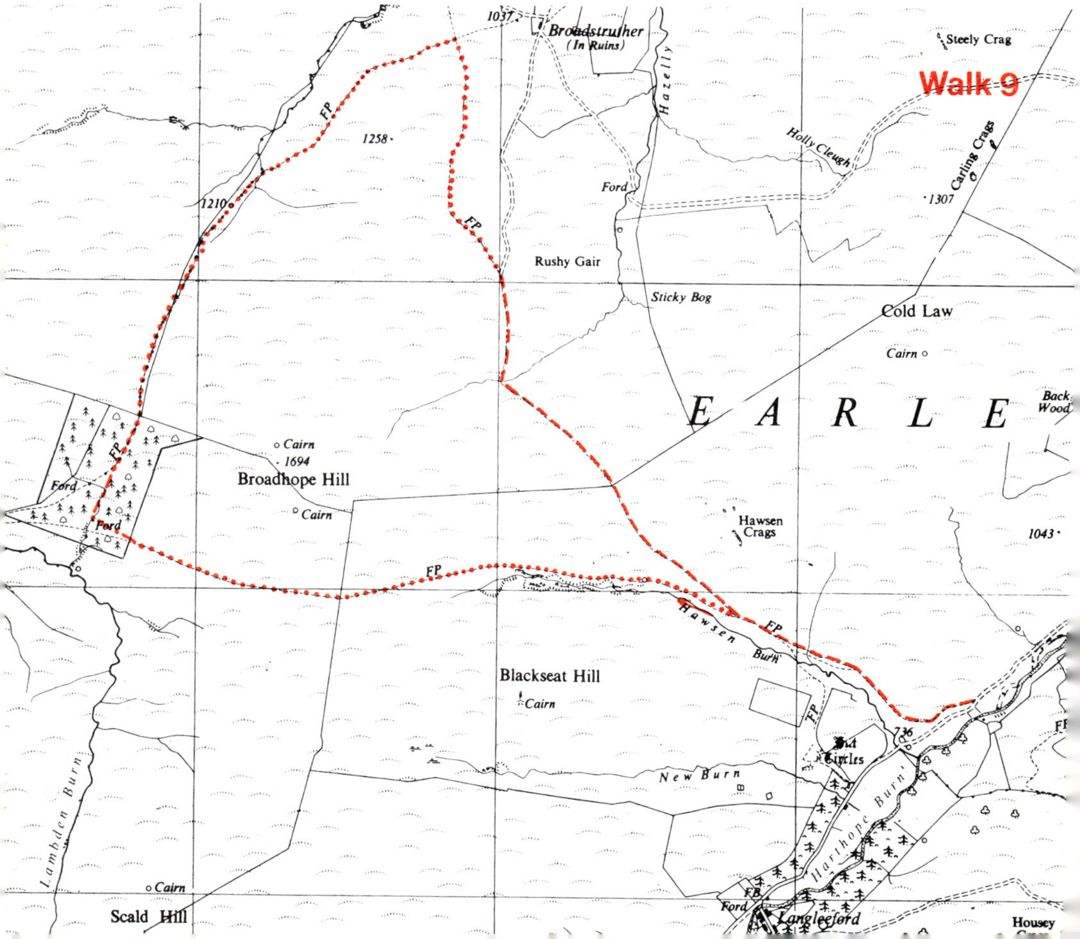

dogs, usually black and white, are bred for speed, intelligence and obedience, and are generally of the Border Collie breed. The first Sheep Dog Trial in England was held in Northumberland in 1876.

For the next mile cairns mark the way to a gate in the fence.

Rushy Gair (L) is aptly named. Gair means a strip of greener, better quality grass and that would have been prized in the days before drainage of these wet moors. The large tussocks of purple moor grass (Molinia caerulea) which make walking so difficult, bear witness to the wet state of the ground. Country people used the long straws of this grass to make brushes, and twisted them together to make a strong or durable line. The grass is named after G. J. Molina, a Spanish botanist of the 18th century who wrote about the plants of Chile.

Cross the stile alongside the gate, beside which is a large stone, possibly a boundary marker. Walk on for a few yards then follow the path below Hawsen Crags (L) and down to the road.

10 Harthope Valley - Carey Burn Bridge - Old Middleton; return via Happy Valley

4 miles, about 2¾ hours. A short climb up on to the hills with good views, then downhill to the hamlet of North Middleton, along a country lane, returning through the pretty Happy Valley.

Cars park on the grassy space (R) just before the first bridge in the valley. Walk back a few yards, pass through the kissing wicket and cross the field. At the gorse bushes look for the stone dyke running downhill (R) and cross the bridge (R) nearby.

Splashes of white on the rocks that litter the fast-flowing burns are a sign that dippers are around. They resemble large wrens and have a distinctive white breast that stands out against the rocks and crags. Their nervous bobbing and conversational song give them an endearing quality; in fact they are very territorial and aggressive towards their neighbours. They feed on aquatic insects by plunging into the water and walking, totally submerged and with wings partly opened, over the slippery boulders.

Walk up the slope and over the stile (L).

The shepherd's cottage which can be seen above the trees (L) bears the strange name of Skirl Naked. Local people call it 'Skirlie'. At the turn of the century there was talk of changing it to Shining Pool, but the old, and certainly original, name remains.

Dipper

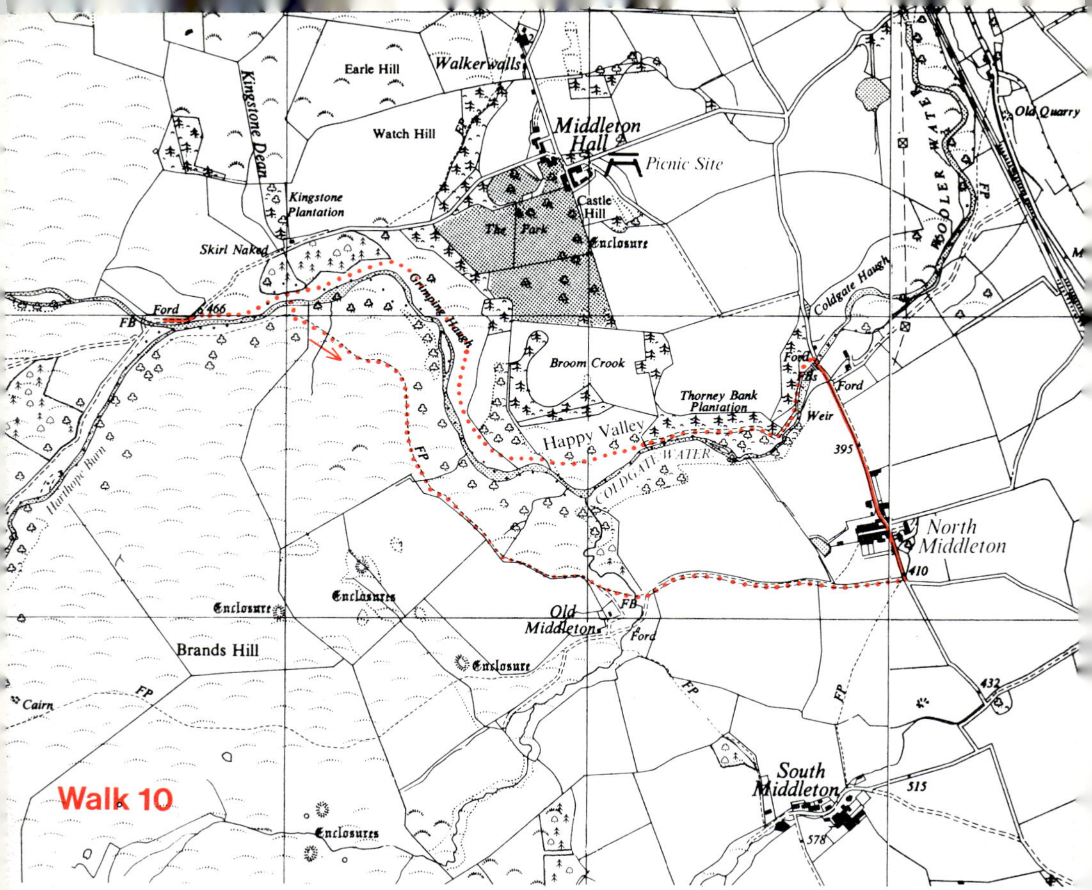

Follow the path up the slope above the pond to the stile in the fence and contour around the hill keeping the fence on the left.

The burn below is Coldgate Water. It began as the Harthope Burn, and a short distance downstream, just past Coldgate Ford, it is called Wooler Water and flows past Wooler to join the River Till. The burns here quite frequently change names on their way to join a larger river.

At the top of the hill turn left and follow the path above the valley, and past the plantation. After the second stile keep to the fence (L) and walk to the bridge.

This bridge was built in 1979 by the National Park Area Warden assisted by a group of Voluntary Wardens. There are about 300 of the latter who patrol well-frequented localities during the holiday season, and who undertake projects such as tree-planting, visitor surveys and litter clearances. There is also an associated Mountain Rescue Team.

Cross the bridge, go up the slope, turn left and follow the track down to the road.

The hamlet seen ahead is North Middleton. Middleton is a very common English place name (Old English 'middel-tun' = 'middle village or homestead') and there are several examples in Northumberland; here there are three – Middleton Hall, North Middleton and South Middleton. In the 13th century this one was known as Middlemost Middleton. The present name dates from the 16th century. These hamlets have a long history. In 1170 Liulf, son of Liulf, was fined for failing to carry wood to the royal beacon at Bamburgh. In 1236 North and South Middleton were held in drengage and truncage to Bamburgh Castle which meant that among other duties the tenant was bound to cart a fixed number of logs to the Castle. Quite an undertaking in those days! By 1686 this had become a money payment of 6s 6d.

Happy Valley – Coldgate Water looking west

Turn left at the road: walk through the hamlet and on to the ford.

Beside the burn is Coldgate Mill (R) which was a corn mill in working order in 1925.

Cross the bridge, turn left and walk into the Happy Valley.

The plantations along this valley are privately owned and used for pheasant rearing and shooting. There is a great variety of trees: Sitka spruce which has a blue look; Norway spruce, the Christmas tree; larch; Scots pine, short needled; Corsican pine, long needled; aromatic Douglas fir and many others, including some deciduous. This interesting mixed woodland admits light and encourages wild life. Siskins, redpolls, goldcrests and long-tailed tits favour the area, as do roe deer. Because the soil is less acid and there are more earthworms, moles are numerous along the woodland pathway. Their hills often indicate a change in the weather; during heavy frosts new tunnel systems are dug to follow the earthworms down into the unfrozen soil.

The path crosses the fields and climbs a slope.

This land belongs to the Middleton Hall Estate. Previous to the 16th century, Middleton Hall was known as North Middleton. It was the place from which the great family of Middleton of Belsay took its name. This family descended from the house of Gospatric which held land here in the 12th century. In 1580 the Scots raided the township and the loss of one of their men, a certain Dandye Dagliesh of Limpetlaw, caused a feud which resulted in further raids in 1588, 1589 and 1597.

The estate passed through various families and in the 17th century was held by Francis Radcliffe, afterwards Earl of Derwentwater.

In 1715, a year after Queen Anne's death, James Radcliffe of Dilston, third Earl of Derwentwater, and grandson of Charles II, joined the Jacobites and marched with the Scots to set James Stuart upon the throne. After their defeat at Preston in Lancashire, the Earl was taken to the Tower of London and beheaded in 1716. The Derwentwater estates were forfeited to the Crown and later used to endow Greenwich Hospital. In 1832 the Hospital Commissioners sold Middleton Hall estate to George Hughes, Lt. Col. of the Royal Cheviot Legion, whose family had long been its tenants. It is said that Happy Valley was given its name by the ladies living at the Hall at the turn of the century.

Follow the haughland back to the parking place.

Bridge across Coldgate Water

South Middleton

This little cluster of cottages, a long way from shops and services, nestles on the lower slopes of the eastern Cheviot foothills, in an area of intensive sheep farming. Its existence was not always so peaceful; it suffered at the hands of the Border Reivers, and in 1579 the Warden of the East March reported that the Scots had raided the hamlet and stolen all the horses.

There is no bus service to South Middleton. Cars should approach it from the A697 south of Wooler, as the ford at Coldgate Mill may cause difficulties. There is no parking space as such, but cars may pull off the road on to the grass opposite the pond at the top of the hamlet. Please take care not to block any field or other entrance, as farm vehicles are always on the move around here.

11 South Middleton - Threestone Burn - The Dod; return via Southmiddletonmoor

6 miles, about 4 hours. A walk into a peaceful part of the Cheviots, with no steep hills to climb. The route follows an unmetalled farm road, then a track across the lower slopes of a hill, returning by a grassy path to rejoin the farm road. Walking boots advisable.

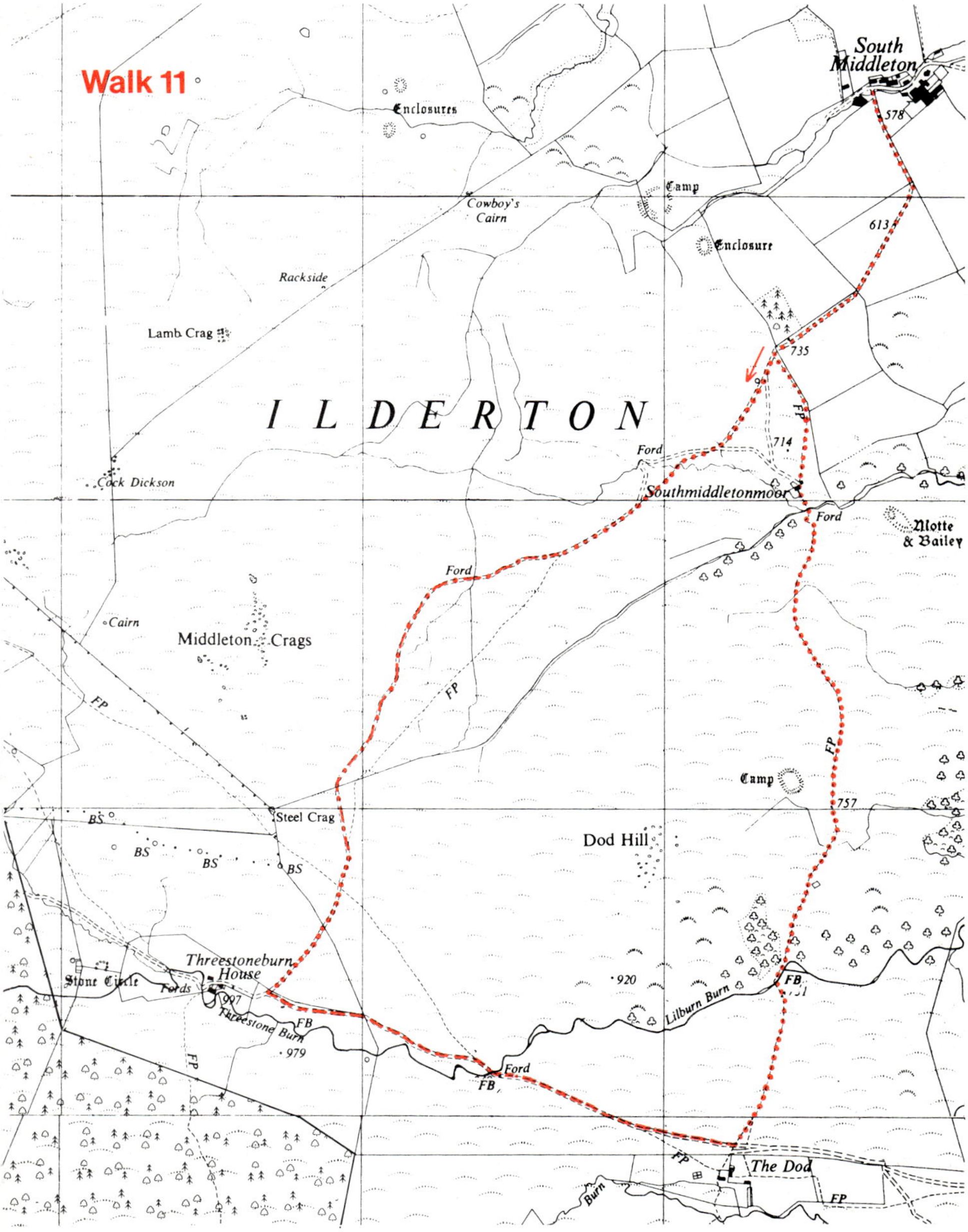

Take the footpath – an unmade road – just below the pond and follow it as far as the plantation (R).

Lapwing, large (12 inches) green-black and white plovers with a long wispy crest, congregate on the arable land especially to the left of the road. Golden plover, beautiful birds with a dark back richly spotted with gold, sometimes visit these fields from their breeding grounds on the high moors.

Lapwing – also known as 'peewit'

Just past the plantation (R) go through the gate (R), walk in front of the stell and on a short distance to pick up the clear, wide farm track which rises gently and runs along the lower slopes of Middleton Crags (R).

Rough moorland such as this provides nesting sites for meadow pipits. The tussocks of purple moor grass (Molinia caerulea) below Dod Hill (L) show that the ground there is wet and peaty.

Leave the track at the point where it turns right and goes uphill, and walk straight on. Go through the gate and follow the sunken, indistinct, rough path.

The upstanding rocks straight ahead are Cunyan Crags. They are a noticeable feature seen against the skyline from the top of Cheviot Street, Wooler. On the other side of the Crags lies the Breamish Valley.

The path leads to a fence and a narrow road.

This is the valley of the Threestone Burn. From Cunyan Crags the land rises to Dunmoor and then to Hedgehope, the second highest hill in the Cheviot range. Forestry Commission plantations cover its side.

Hedgehope Hill from Threestoneburn Photograph by J. R. Hope

Just beyond Threestoneburn House and the trees beside it (R) is a stone circle which may have been built in the Bronze Age. Few of its stones remain standing. Years ago a flint knife was found within the circle.

Over the ridge beyond the house to the right of Hedgehope, lies Langleeford in the Harthope Valley.

Turn left and walk along the road to the farm – The Dod – (R) and follow the path (L) opposite the last of the sheep pens. Pass by the rocks (L) and go on to cross the burn by the bridge.

Not far from here the Threestone Burn changes its name to Lilburn Burn and flows on to join the River Till. Alders line its banks, as they do so many of the burns, flourishing in the damp soil at the sides of rocky streams.

Walk up the slope to the left hand corner of the fence and go along beside it passing just below the rounded knoll (R).

A saucer shaped enclosure, possibly Romano-British, as it does not seem to be situated with defence purposes in mind, is a few yards to the left of the path.

Notice straight ahead the top of a plantation showing above green slopes. Walk in that direction and soon the cottage of Southmiddletonmoor will be in sight. Cross the burn opposite the cottage, walk up the slope and just to the right of the buildings. The footpath runs along the grassy slope to the right of the road and after a short distance it meets it near the plantation. Follow the road back to South Middleton.

Common alder – leaves and cones

Kirknewton

This attractive village nestling at the foot of the hills was called New Town in 1336. It suffered repeatedly from depredations by the Scots during the years of Border raids. A tower of refuge was in existence in 1415 and was still standing in 1554.

The church has a curious low, vaulted chancel. The older part is principally 13th century. Set in the wall by the chancel is a strange carving, thought to be 12th century, of the Adoration of the Magi, with the Wise Men dressed in kilts. In the church yard is the tomb of Josephine Butler, the great Victorian social reformer.

There is a bus service from Wooler once a week, on Saturday.

There is no car park, but just to the east of the church the main road has a grass verge.

12 Kirknewton-Hethpool Bell; return via Torlee House and Old Yeavering

4 miles, about 2¾ hours. A pleasant walk with no steep hills to climb, only a short scramble down a grassy bank at one point. The path runs beside, then above, the College Burn, crosses it at a picturesque spot and takes the walker along level ground below Easter Tor and Yeavering Bell. The last half mile follows the road.

Leave cars on the grass verge beside the main B6351 road, just to the east of the church. Walk along the road, westwards, for a short distance, as far as the old railway house (R).

The railway line from Alnwick to Cornhill, opened on 5th September 1887, ran along here. Catastrophic floods in 1948 severed the line between Wooler and Alnwick and that part of the line closed in 1953. The northern section – Wooler to Cornhill and serving Kirknewton – closed for passenger traffic in 1930, but survived for goods until March 1965.

Just past the house take the footpath (L) which runs along the right hand edge of the field.

The small arches each side of the main one carrying the bridge over the burn enable flood water to drain away. Do not be alarmed if you see bulls in this or the next field. Hill farmers with only a small amount of good quality pasture have at times to put their beef bulls on it. Walk quietly without fuss, and the bull will only cast a casual glance, if that.

The path leads to a gate (R) which gives access to the bridge over the College Burn.

In 1556 this burn was called 'Colleche', a name perhaps derived from the Anglo-Saxon 'col' and 'leche' meaning a stream flowing through boggy land.

Cross the bridge and turn left.

During the summer viper's bugloss (Echium vulgare) flowers here, making a splash of vivid blue. It likes dry, bare and waste places such as this.

Walk a few yards beside the burn, then go up the slope and over the ladder stile, following the path above the trees.

Green woodpeckers like these old oaks and other deciduous trees because of the insects they harbour, and their loud, ringing 'laugh' is often heard.

The path leads to a gate in the wall.

The trees (R) are the Collingwood Oaks on Hethpool Bell. Admiral Collingwood who inherited the Hethpool Estate through his wife, was raised to the peerage for his services at the battle of Trafalgar, 1805, and took the title of Baron Collingwood of Hethpool and Coldburn. Although Hethpool was not his main residence he took a great interest in the estate, and planted many oaks

Green woodpecker

which he hoped would grow into fine timber for his ships.

In 1980 the Northumberland National Park took over the management of this grove, in order to preserve and regenerate the trees. The fence was erected to keep out sheep and cattle which would destroy young seedlings.

Straight ahead is Hethpool House built in 1919 on the site of one erected in 1687. By the small red-roofed building at the end of the garden is the ivy-covered ruin of a pele tower, built in 1415 as a place of refuge in times of raid. A survey of the Border in 1541 described this pele as a 'lytle stone house or pyle which ys a greate releyffe to the tennants thereof'. No doubt it was, because Hethpool suffered repeatedly at the hands of the Scottish Reivers from the 13th century. As late as 1596 a band of Kerrs, Youngs and Burns descended on the village and stole 40 cows and oxen, killing a man in the process.

The Collingwood Oaks

Bridge over the College Burn

Turn left, down the grassy bank, to cross the bridge (L).

A few minutes rest on this bank may reward one with a glimpse of the Cheviot wild goats which roam the hills across the burn. These animals, which cannot be approached closely, are feral, as the true wild goat has never been an indigenous British mammal. Perhaps they are the descendants of goats placed on the hillsides by shepherds centuries ago.

Over the bridge turn left, cross the stile and walk uphill and straight on for a short distance to pick up a path which leads to an easy crossing of the gully (L). Walk towards the wall of the field and keep it on your left hand as far as Torleehouse.

This shepherd's cottage, once known as 'Tarleazes' was so called because the land is a clearing on a hill.

Follow the track in front of the cottage and on to the houses at Old Yeavering.

Yeavering Bell (R) has upon its summit the remains of the largest prehistoric hill fort in Northumberland. Within the encircling stone ramparts there were at least 130 timber built huts, their sites now marked by slight crescent-shaped scoops and platforms.

The Bell is another favourite haunt of wild goats.

Walk across the field at Old Yeavering and pass in front of the cottages.

It was long thought that this was the site of the 7th century palace of King Edwin of Northumbria, but aerial photography in 1950 revealed unusual crop markings in the field across the main road. A three year dig disclosed the original timber post holes and the site of a wooden amphitheatre. A memorial at the roadside a short distance to the east of the cottages tells the story.

At the main road turn left for Kirknewton.

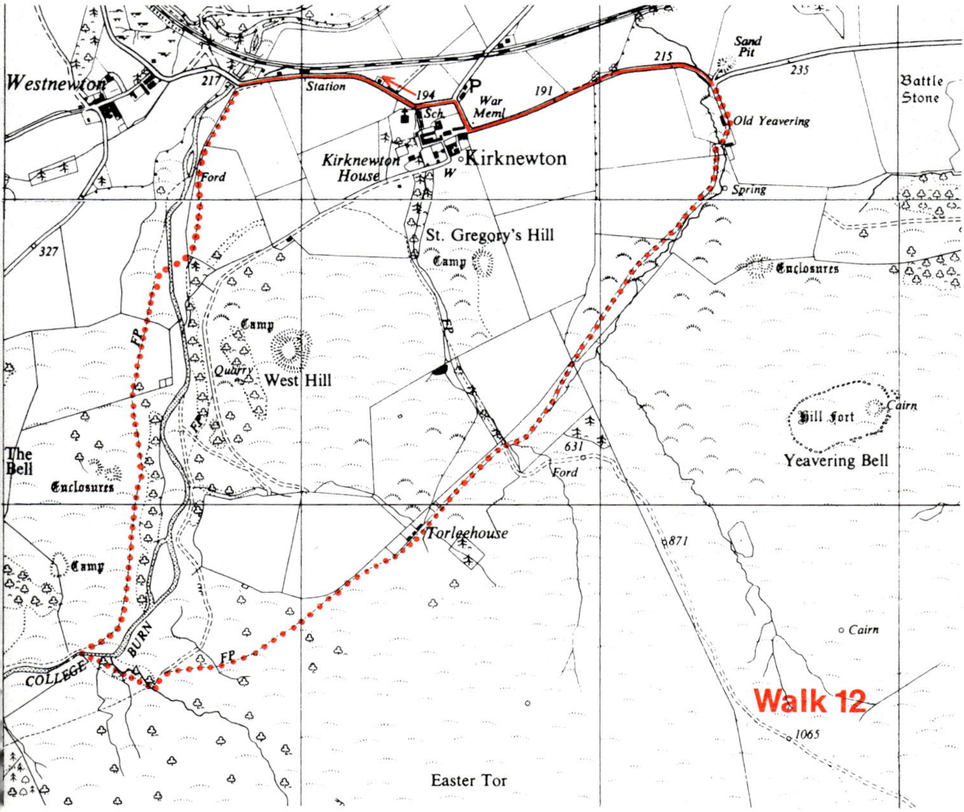

The College Valley

This beautiful unspoilt valley, enclosed by high hills, runs right up to the western side of The Cheviot. Formed by a geological fault, it was later, during the Ice Ages, scoured out by ice flowing from the top of The Cheviot. The meltwater from small glaciers flowing off the rounded hill summits carried pebbles and sand and deposited them along the valley floor; this can be seen as gravel terraces left above the present river course.

Although the College Valley is always open to walkers, only 12 cars per day are permitted to drive further than Hethpool, and during the lambing season, from approximately 12th April to 12th May, no cars are allowed. The free permit is obtained from John Sale and Partners, Estate Agents, 18 Glendale Road, Wooler. Only one walk in this book, that from Mounthooly at the head of the valley, requires a permit. There is no bus service to Hethpool.

13 The College Valley - Elsdonburn - The Scottish Border; return via Trowupburn

5 miles, about 3½ hours. A fine, clear day is best for this bracing walk with its superlative views of the Scottish Borderlands. No very steep hills to climb, but walking boots advisable.

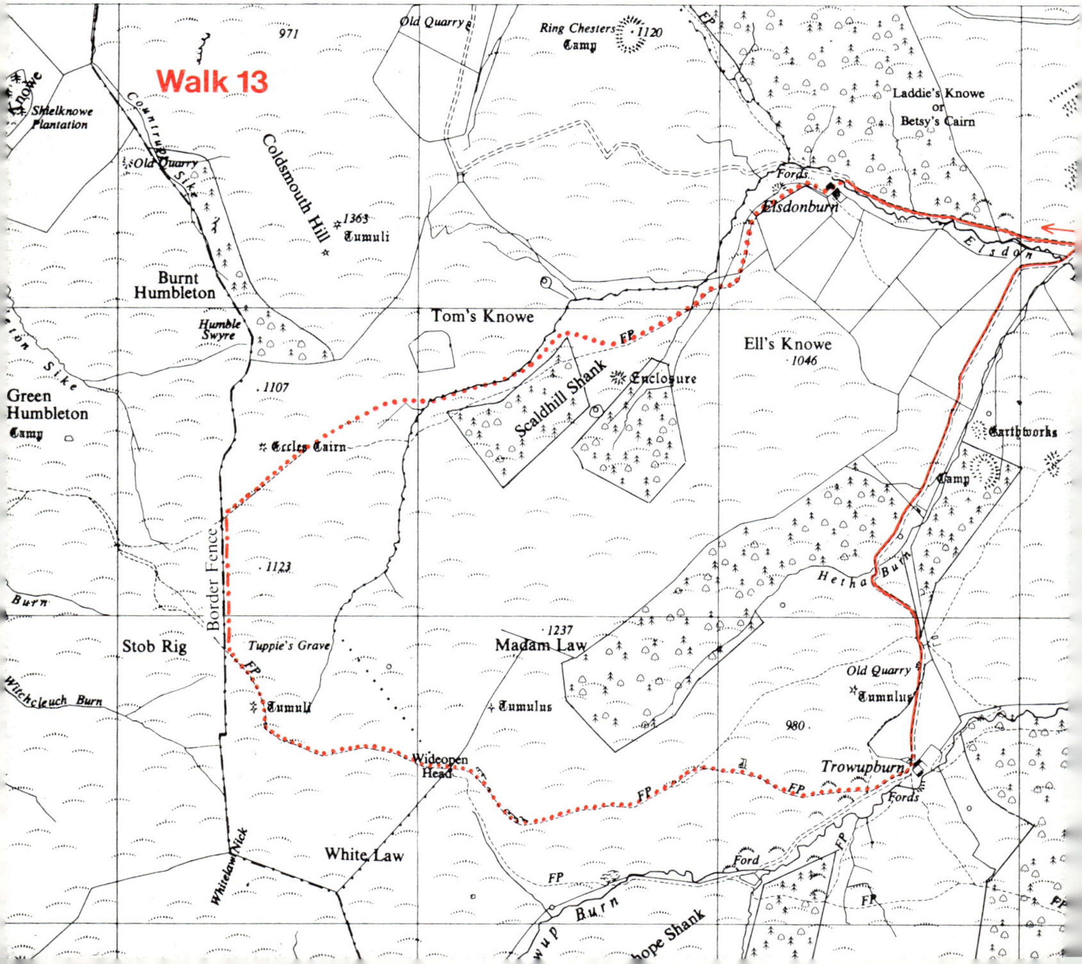

Leave the main road at Westnewton and drive towards Hethpool. About 1¼ miles along the road, at the point where it bends left to enter Hethpool, take the road (R) which is gated. Please close this gate behind you. Drive to the fork and park the car on the grass. Walk about ¼ mile along the road to the farm seen ahead, and follow the track (L).

This is Elsdonburn. Seen through the trees in front of the bungalow are Easter and Wester Tors.

Pass around the bungalow, go through the gate and follow the track to the next gate. A few steps past this second gate, taking the track (R), cross the burn, walk up the slope, through the gate and across the field.

From Elsdonburn looking east to Easter Tor (L) and Wester Tor

The large saucer-shaped enclosure (L) dates possibly from Romano-British times when there was less need for fortified encampments on high ground.

At the plantation turn right, walk to its lower edge and then turn left, keeping above the burn.

The small, stone building in the walled enclosure (R) was no doubt used in the past by shepherds staying out with their lambing flock.

At the end of the plantation, cross the burn by the planks (R), walk up the slope and then bear slightly left up the hill. Notice the small rounded summit between the hills more or less straight ahead. Walk towards it.

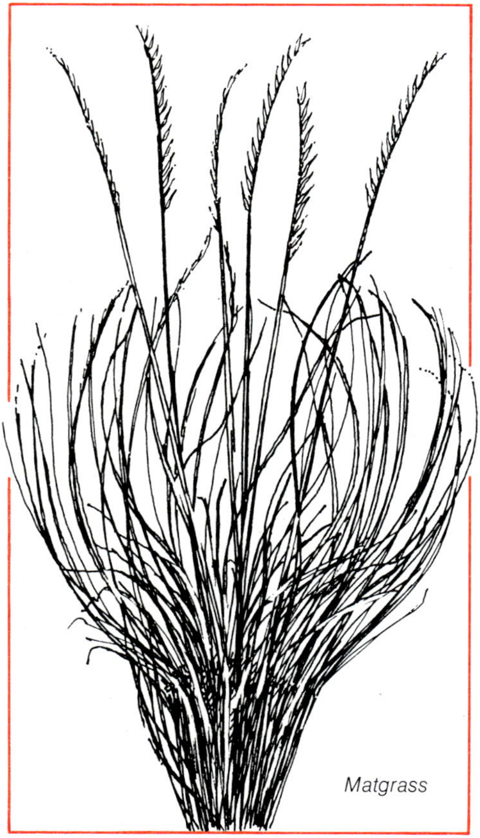

Matgrass

Much of the grass on these hills is matgrass (Nardus stricta) which differs from all our native grasses in that in June it bears an erect, unbranched spike with spikelets arranged in two rows on one side of the spike and always pointing one way. Little clumps of this grass can often be found blowing around.

Areas of matgrass bleach almost white at the end of summer, giving rise to the name 'The White Lands'.

On reaching the level ground, turn left to go around the hillock.

Eccles Cairn (R) was doubtless the burial place of a prehistoric chieftain. The stones have obviously been removed, perhaps to build the nearby dyke. This is the Border between England and Scotland. Below is Green Humbleton encircled by the ramparts and ditches of a prehistoric encampment. Town Yetholm is beyond, with the church and rooftops of Kirk Yetholm just visible in front. The Yetholms were the headquarters of the Faa gipsies who used to pasture their horses below the Border Fence. The last 'Queen' of the gipsies died in 1883, and a little house in Kirk Yetholm is called 'The Gipsy Palace'. In the distance are the three peaks of the Eildon Hills near Melrose.

Walk to the gate, but remain on the English side.

For something like 400 years, from the 13th century to after the Union of the Crowns in 1603, the whole of the Border from the Solway Firth to Berwick upon Tweed was an area of lawlessness. The 16th century saw the heyday of the Border Reivers, members of the big English and Scottish families or 'Riding Surnames', among them Armstrong, Foster, Hall, Carleton, Kerr, Scott, etc. Men of the Riding Surnames were known by their nick-names; in state papers one reads of Archie 'Fire the Braes', Jock 'Stowlugs', Davie 'Bangtaile', 'Red-Neb Hob', 'Nebless Clemmie' and Kinmont Willie whose name has gone down into history because of his daring rescue from Carlisle Castle by the Bold Buccleugh. Sir Walter Scott was a descendant of 'Auld Wat' of Harden. Entangled in a web of intermarriage and deadly feud, the loyalty of the Riding Surnames was always questionable.

Knowing every inch of these hills, the Reivers rode mainly by moonlight in the autumn, to descent upon a household or hamlet and drive off the horses and cattle, often with burning and bloodshed.

By the law of 'Hot Trod' the victim could seek immediate redress by giving chase with his friends, riding with horn and hound and hue and cry, and with a burning turf on the lance point. This could cause retaliation and it was often safer to rob someone else instead. In one raid in Tynedale three cattle were stolen. Joined by his friends and some neighbouring garrison troops, the victim made a Hot Trod, failed to recover his goods, turned asied to raid in his turn, and returned home with 300 cattle!

Turn left, walk beside the Border Fence (R) to the next gate (R).

The signpost assists walkers on the Pennine Way fair weather route to or from Kirk Yetholm. This ancient Border crossing, known as the White Swire, was mentioned in a Royal Command of 1222 when Henry III ordered the Sheriff of Northumberland and the Bishop of Durham to journey here to settle the Marches between England and Scotland, restoring them to their status in the time of King John and his predecessors.

At the gate turn left and follow the path above the burn head (L) to the gate, and on along the middle slopes of the hill (L). The path goes around the hill, by the large stone-walled enclosure (L) and down to the farm.

The Cheviot Hills were once known as the Forest of Cheviot. This meant-not necessarily a wooded area, but a hunting ground within which the forest laws applied. In spite of the common pastures situated in the 'forést' wild game was preserved, and one of the laws stated that all dogs used otherwise than for the chase, had to have one foot shortened to prevent their disturbing the game. In 1168 the Forester Ralph, son of Main, accounted for 22s 10d in fines from the men of Northumberland who had not shortened the feet of their dogs.

Walk along the farm road by the buildings (R). Please close all gates.

This is Trowupburn. In King John's reign the land, then called 'Trolhopeburn' was given to Melrose Abbey by Robert Muschampe; a charter allowed the monastery's servants to use mastiffs for shepherding, but to control them by the blowing of horns.

On the 11th of June 1596 there was a visit from the Border Reivers and 80 sheep were stolen.

The road leads back to the starting point.

View south from Eccles Cairn

14 The College Valley - Mounthooly - Red Cribs; return via The Schil and Fleehope Burn

5 miles, about 3½ hours. A lovely drive along the College Valley for which a permit is required; see notes at beginning of section on The College Valley. Take care on the narrow road, especially at Fleehope. This is an exciting walk along part of the Pennine Way on the Scottish Border, in an area steeped in history. Some hills to climb. Pick a fine, clear day to enjoy the wonderful views. Walking boots advisable.

Leave cars on the grass before the gate at Mounthooly; walk along the road, pass the shepherd's bungalow (L) and follow the track up the valley. Notice the reddish gash in the hillside straight ahead: the path goes just to the right of it. Walk to the right of the stell opposite the last plantation (R) and keep to the lower slopes of the hill: then climb up with the gully (L).

Red Cribs, named perhaps after the colour of the soil, was mentioned in 1597 as 'Gribbheade, a passage and hyeway for the theefe'. There are signs of an old trackway or drove road.

Walk across to the Border Fence.

Before the Union of the Crowns in 1603 the Border was divided on both sides into the East, Middle and West Marches. Each March

The College Valley from the Pennine Way

was in the charge of a Warden who attempted to keep order in his area, and that was no easy task. A Memorandum of 1579 stated that the 'decay' of the English Marches was due to raids by the Scots, neglect of horses and arms, castles and forts in unworthy hands, and deadly private feuds. A Warden, reporting to the government in London in 1583, complained of difficulties in carrying out his duties, as the following families were at feud: the Armstrongs, Crosiers, Elwoods, Erringtons, Fenwicks, Herons, Nixons, Olivers, Shaftoes, Trumbles and Withringtons. Intermarrying and feuding resulted in raids by both English and Scots, in which the Wardens themselves frequently participated.

The short, steep slope (L) leads to Auchope Cairn at the western end of the summit of The Cheviot, the highest hill of the range. Carved

into its flank (L) is Henhole, a corrie and gorge sculptured from the rocks during the Ice Age. The College Burn rises at the head of Henhole and cascades down in a series of waterfalls.

There are many legends about Henhole; fairies were said to live in the mossy clefts by the falls; huntsmen were lured to their death by mysterious music, and Black Adam, a notorious freebooter, had his lair in the gorge. On one occasion he burst in upon a wedding party at Wooperton, robbed the guests and stabbed the bride. Pursued by the bridegroom he rode back to Henhole, but in attempting to jump the gorge, both men fell to their deaths on the rocks below.

Years ago some massive mountings of late Celtic bronze harness and horse trappings were found in a nearby bank of clay.

The railway wagon just across the Border Fence, in Scotland, is the Pennine Way shelter. It has proved a blessing, indeed often a life-saver, to long distance walkers who have had a gruelling slog of nearly 25 miles across the highest, wildest and most remote part of the Cheviots, often in bad weather.

Turn right and walk along the Pennine Way, beside the Border Fence, to the rocky summit of the Schil.

To the south is the long hill of Windy Gyle, at 2,032 feet the third highest in the range, with a large cairn known as Russell's Cairn on its summit. This cairn is probably the burial place of a prehistoric chieftain, but its name is derived from an incident in the days of the Border troubles. In July 1585 the English

Henhole from the Pennine Way

and Scottish Wardens of the Middle Marches met on the lower northern slopes of Windy Gyle, near Hexpethgate where the old drove road, 'Clennel Street', passes from Scotland into England. While they were conducting the day's business – settling disputes and trying felons – a shot rang out and an Englishman, Lord Francis Russell, fell dead. The English blamed the Scots; the Scots blamed an English youth who had stolen some spurs. In accordance with 'Jeddart Justice' (hang first, try later) the boy was immediately hanged, but the murderer of Lord Francis Russell was never found.

The Pennine Way runs from the top of The Cheviot, past Hexpethgate, and on beside Russell's Cairn.

This long distance walk way, some 270 miles from Edale in Derbyshire to Kirk Yetholm in

Waterfalls at the Henhole

Scotland, was the inspiration of Mr. Tom Stephenson of the Ramblers' Association. He fought for many years to establish this, the second longest footpath in Britain and the first to be completed as the result of proposals made by the National Parks Commission (now the Countryside Commission). It was opened in 1965.

Follow the Pennine Way up the Schil, descend the other side, go through a gate and walk on to the ladder stile (L).

The Pennine Way crosses this stile into Scotland and leads on to Kirk Yetholm, 6 miles away.

Turn right, walk on a few yards then bear

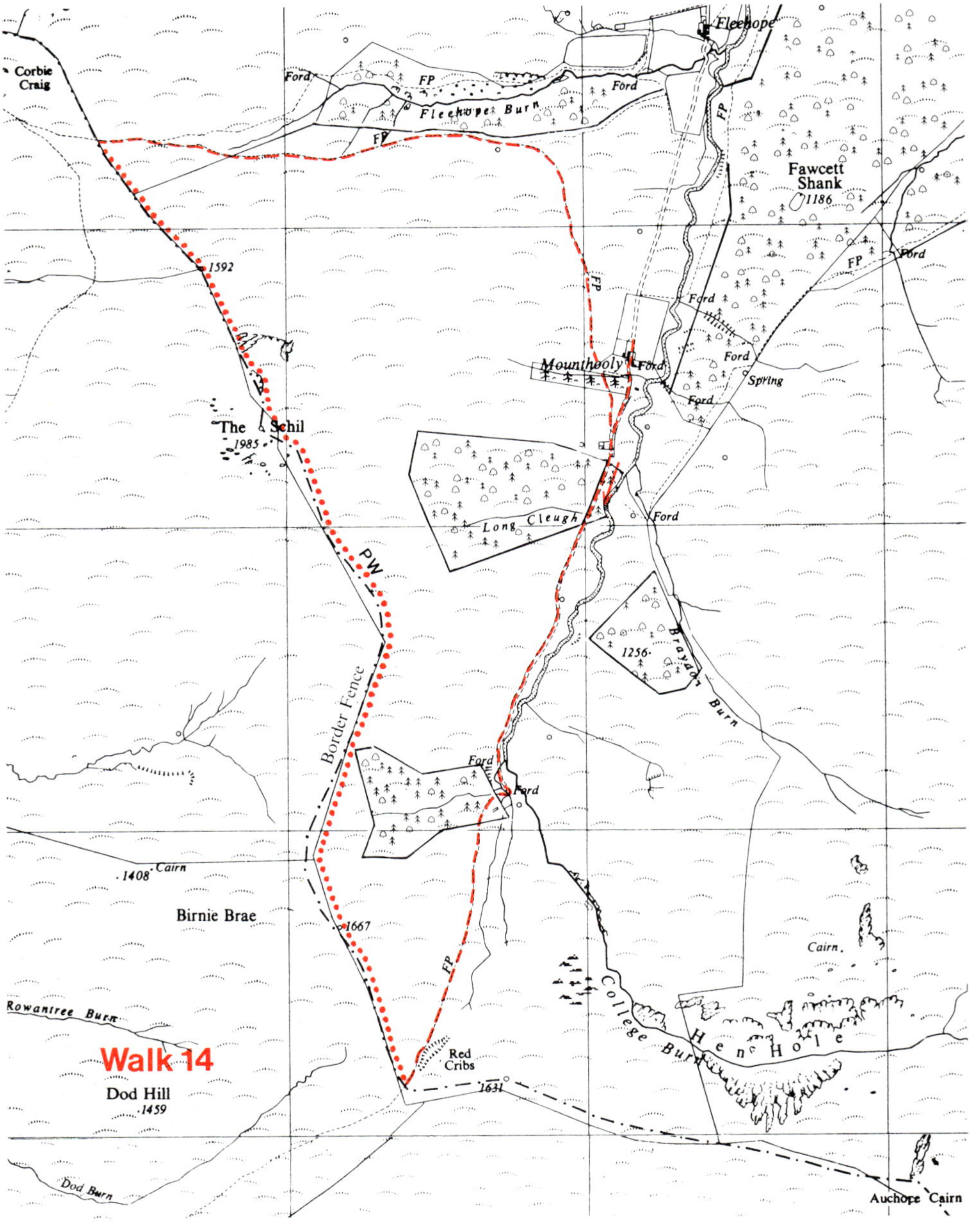

slightly right towards the fence, leaving the rushes just to the left.

These rushes indicate wet soil; this is the source of the Fleehope Burn. Ring ouzels, the mountain blackbird, breed among the heather and rocks beside these hill burns, usually above 1,000 feet. The male is black with a broad, white crescent across the breast. Ring ouzels winter around the Mediterranean.

Go through the gate, cross the rough ground, keeping the plantation on the left. A path soon appears, passing a stell (R).

The Fleehope Burn and the farmstead lie below (L). The name is perhaps derived from the old word 'fleog', a fly; the valley where flies were troublesome. In 1556 Sir John Forster leased the land of 'Fleope' at a quarterly rent of 20s. In the 17th century the lands were shiels, or summer grazing grounds.

Although many burns and sikes drain into the valley, it is not subjected to 'flash floods' because the depth of peat on The Cheviot and surrounding hills absorbs even heavy rain and snowfall like a sponge, and releases the water gradually.

Follow the path as it bears right and goes downhill. At the gate, turn left for the road.

The acorn– the Countryside Commission's long distance footpath waymark.

Ring Ouzel

Glossary

Some unusual or difficult words used in this book – approximate pronunciations are given where appropriate

Bell	Hill
Cairn	A pile of stones to mark a prehistoric burial site, or a route
Cist (Kist)	Prehistoric stone coffin or burial chamber
Cleugh (Cluff)	Ravine
Corrie	Circular hollow on a hillside
Dyke	Wall
Glidders	Scree; a slope of loose rocks
Haugh (Harf)	Flat ground by a stream
Heugh (Heeuff)	A hill which ends abruptly
Hole	Hollow
Hope	A strip of better land in a narrow valley. (This was a desirable possession. In 1315 John Comyn left in his will, 'a certain number of hopes in Northumberland')
Knowe (Now)	Hillock; applied to lesser hills and moorland slopes
Law	Hill
Leat	Open watercourse carrying water to a mill
Lough (Loff)	Lake
Reiver	Robber
Romano-British	At the time of the Roman occupation of Britain
Shiel	A summer grazing ground; a circular timber and turf hut on such a ground. The word is still used for fishermen's huts
Sike	Small stream
Stell	A circular enclosure of stone for sheltering sheep
Swire	A neck of land
Trows (sound as in now)	Troughs or little valleys
Villein	A feudal serf, entirely subject to the Lord of the Manor

Looking north-east into the National Park from Eccles Cairn

For further reading

LIFE AND DEATH IN PREHISTORIC NORTHUMBERLAND
by Stan Beckensall
Frank Graham, 1976

*ROCKS AND SCENERY FROM TYNE TO TWEED
by C. R. Warn
Frank Graham, 1975

*A GUIDE TO THE GEOLOGY OF THE CHEVIOT HILLS
by D. A. Robson
Transactions of the Natural History Society of Northumbria
Vol. 43, No 1, 1976

THE SCOTTISH BORDER AND NORTHUMBERLAND
by J. Talbot White
Eyre Methuen Ltd., 1973

THE STEEL BONNETS
by G. McDonald Fraser
Barrie and Jenkins Ltd., 1971 and Pan Books Ltd., 1974

*NORTHUMBERLAND – NATIONAL PARK GUIDE NO. 7
Edited by J. Philipson
H.M.S.O., 1969

Titles marked * are available from the National Park Information Centre, Ingram

The Border Fence